TRAIN YOUR HUMAN

TRAIN YOUR HUMAN
A Manual for Caring Dogs

Bonzo 'Good Boy' Jones

With additional information for owners

DAVID & CHARLES
NEWTON ABBOT   LONDON   NORTH POMFRET (Vt)

British Library Cataloguing in Publication Data

Loxton, Howard
   Train your human.
   I. Title
   828'.9'1408   PN6175

   ISBN 0-7153-7678-0

Library of Congress Catalog Card
Number 78-74087

Typeset and printed in Great Britain
by Biddles Ltd, Guildford, Surrey
for David & Charles (Publishers) Limited
Brunel House Newton Abbot Devon

Published in the United States of America
by David & Charles Inc
North Pomfret Vermont 05053. USA

CONTENTS

PUBLISHER'S NOTE

Bonzo 'Good Boy' Jones' introduction to the basics of human training and manipulation has been available to dogs for a number of years, but few people today have the necessary linguistic ability to read it in its original form, compiled as it is on an interesting variety of materials and carved in diverse canine media of which tooth and claw are only two. Nevertheless, it has long had the reputation among dog trainers and veterinary surgeons of being a veritable bible for those who wish to understand dog care and maintenance in depth; who wish to bring to the field a genuinely informed view, the truly canine view.

We feel, therefore, a certain degree of justifiable pride in publishing the first English edition of this expert work, and in making it available and accessible to the human public at large. Certain compromises have had to be made—for example, there is no English translation of the canine term for which the word 'owner' has been used— but these have been kept to a minimum.

We hope that this publication will provide a valuable service to dogs and humans alike; if it assists in even the smallest of ways towards making the man-dog relationship a happier and more productive one, then our task, and that of the translator, will have been worth while.

The tables on pages 39–41 were compiled by Dr A. D. Walker, ACIS, MIBiol, FRIC, FIFST.

PREFACE

My owner's shelves are full of books written about dogs from the human point of view, many of them by authors with considerable understanding of our needs who have sought to promote a happy dog-human relationship, but until now I do not believe that much has appeared presenting the partnership from our point of view. Indeed, my limited researches have found only one case of dog authorship reaching publication, and that a rather sycophantic letter-writer called Nero whose collection of rather trivial epistles to his master, Thomas Carlyle, appeared on the bookstalls more than a century ago.* It seems time to redress the balance and to give canines some help in coping with human beings and to guide them in securing a way of life worthy of an intelligent dog.

This is not a book designed to show every young pup how to get his own way, for enjoyable though that might be for a time it could have disastrous results: a life without restraint would soon become an unhappy and an unhealthy one. Moderation, understanding and a willingness to reach a compromise will get further than viciousness or bullying in relationships with humans as with other animals.

I am an old dog now, and have lived parts of my life with very different owners, but what I write is not only the result of my experience for it draws upon the observations of my many friends (and some dogs whom I hesitate to

---

*My own opinion is that these letters are a forgery perpetrated by Mr Carlyle's wife.

name as such) who over the years have passed on their own knowledge of the human world. I hope that this book will set any young pup upon the road to a fulfilling life and that, if it should fall into the hands of an owner, it will teach the humans a little more about the dog-human partnership and how to ensure the greatest happiness for both animals.

B. 'G.B.' J.

1 THE CANINE HERITAGE

Dogs have been around for thousands if not millions of years. We are descended from the same early ancestors as the cats, the bears and a number of other remote relations whom no self-respecting canine need feel obliged to recognize. The cats rapidly evolved into something very like their present-day form and, in their self-centred, feline-headed way, have refused to change. Some of their human patrons claim that this is because they evolved in such a well-balanced, sophisticated way that they could not improve themselves any further: you have only to think of those you know, whether lion, tiger or the domestic tabby with which we often share the hearth to realize that this is nonsense.

We, on the other hand, took time to perfect ourselves. Several regional variations and forms adapted to particular environments went their own ways, and it is possible that the wolf and the jackal may be the immediately preceding stages in our evolutionary development, although there is no clear evidence to show the truth. Humans had not then developed their technique of writing to act as our historians, and pack tradition has not preserved any clear race memory of those early times, except in so far as it is possible to have successful matings with the wolf and some lesser species. Perhaps there is a 'missing-link' still to be discovered between the prehistoric and the modern dog. No doubt, one day, some human professor will make it his life's work to discover it.

Equally unknown, and obscured by innumerable myths,

is the story of the beginning of our special relationship with man. Individuals of other species have sometimes had a close rapport with humans, and many have been exploited for the benefit of *Homo sapiens,* but it is only we who have this true bond of loyalty and understanding—is it too sentimental and old–fashioned to call it love?—with man. Some cats, especially those under the influence of canine *mores*, approach it, but their relationship with humans is of comparatively recent origin and, even were their basic character less introverted, they have so recently been considered instruments of the devil by many large groups of humans, who tortured and persecuted them, that one can hardly expect them to be able to extend the deep cross–species trust of which we are capable. Indeed, you could have a worse aim in life than to educate the felines in your domestic pack to a true belief in human goodness and forgiveness for past human errors.

Dogs around the world all tell their own legends to explain our partnership with man. In the Chittagong hills of eastern India the packs used to tell how God made the world, the trees and the animals, leaving the human man and woman until the last. He slept before he had finished his hominids and, during his sleep, a great snake came curving by and ate them. This happened several times so God asked the dog to stand guard while he slept. The snake dared not approach and in the morning the finishing touches were given to the human male and female. Since then man has been dependent upon the protection and patronage of the dog and even in the wild it has been the dog's duty to howl or bark a warning to any humans who may be in earshot when danger threatens. From other places too come variations of this legend of God placing man in our protection.

Another story, from Indonesia, tells how the dog dug a hole in the ground and discovered the first man and woman. Delightfully though they express the closeness of our feelings, we must discount those legends by which various American Indian tribes attributed their origins to matings between dog and woman, or bitch and man. It is not conceivable that successful matings could have taken place—at least there is no recorded historical example of them being successful and human biologists agree in this. We must see this as an example of humans who, more than most, appreciated the nobility of the dog, wishing through such symbolic magic to share in it.

Human dependence upon canines is a theme repeated in stories such as that of Romulus and Remus, whom one of our wolf sisters reared that they might live to found the city of Rome. Another such story comes from Sarawak where dogs remember how they noticed the way in which creepers moving in the wind rubbed against the trunk of a tree, producing heat at the spot; by drawing man's attention to what was happening they enabled humans to make fire, so that we might all warm ourselves. A tale told by Red Indian humans says that at creation man was on one side of a chasm and all the other animals on the other. The dog alone took a great run and, leaping, threw himself across the void. His front paws just gripped the opposite edge and man held him and pulled him up. No other animals had the courage to follow and so man and dog became friends, separate from all other living creatures.

Of course, nothing so romantic as all these stories is likely to be the real explanation (although the origin of fire has a ring of truth). Our ancestors probably took advantage of man's hunting efforts to steal some of the kill for themselves. When man lit his fires, which probably kept most animals away, we risked the burning danger and shared in the security and warmth given by the flames. Gradually, man saw how helpful we could be to him and began to welcome us, freely offering part of his catch in return for our help in hunting and the warning which we gave of any danger. Even in those early days man's senses had probably deteriorated to well below the levels of ours—the price the humans have had to pay for the extra paw dexterity and other assets which they have.

Perhaps it was ambitious dogs, not yet able to have their

own pack, who first made the move to the human camp; perhaps whole packs lived on the fringes, gradually gaining a greater mutual tolerance and understanding with the humans. Certainly our bitches began to use the humans' caves and huts to have their pups, and the pups began to play with the human young.

It must have become apparent quite early on that there were some things that humans are better at than we are—and on those matters dogs were prepared to fall in with a man's plans. Since we had joined his pack it was also natural that we should follow his pack leader rather than plan separate strategies. Later, when humans began to live in much smaller—family—packs, more like our own, we tended to adopt a single human in the group as pack leader and to ignore the wider administration, a situation much closer to the close-knit dependence but general freedom of our natural pack structure.

Some strange things happened in the early times of our relationship with man. In some places he worshipped us as gods, in others he put us in his cooking pot. Most far-reaching in its effects, he began to interfere in our sex life; especially that of our bitches. He prevented some dogs from mating with them and carefully chose fathers for a particular bitch's pups to ensure that certain traits and certain strains would be emphasized. Had it not been for man's interference, we might today have had as widely varied a mixture of type, colour and conformation as the humans themselves have. Instead the clearly defined breeds of today emerged and, although their members may not personally care much for their ancestry (except perhaps for some of those snooty Afghans), they should be aware of the very great effect this interference has had on the forming of their character and physique.

Some breeds have been almost unchanged for thousands of years, others are of very recent origin. Whatever your personal feelings about miscegenation it is worth remembering that many humans set great store by pure breeding and long pedigrees. Even men and women who are quite without any racial prejudice or class consciousness where their own species are concerned can feel quite strongly about the need for us to maintain pure blood lines. Whatever your feelings may be, in principle their attitude does become possible to understand when you see a particularly fine example of a dog or bitch of a certain physical form and aptitude. One's admiration alone prompts the wish that a union should be arranged which would reproduce a comparable excellence. This is a subject of interest and controversy to which I shall return, but I would ask impatient young dogs to consider for a moment and appreciate that, by his interference, man has helped us elevate our natural lustfulness into a form of art.

We dogs have always prided ourselves upon our steadfast loyalty. Our association with man has inevitably undermined this somewhat, for he will attach his loyalty to so many pointless human ideas outside the pack—to gods, to political, financial or other abstract groupings—typical of a brain that spends so much time thinking about crazy ideas instead of concentrating on such healthy issues as food, sex, exercise and other sensual satisfactions. It is up to us all to set the humans a good example.

The fineness of our senses also sets us above the humans and all dogs should take care to exercise them and keep them sharp. It is all too simple to have an easy life, relying upon others or upon mechanical devices to monitor the world around us, but that can lead only to atrophy, as it has in man. Humans cannot see, hear, smell or feel pressure properly—and it is only our example that makes them realize how sadly inefficient they are. Without us they might well have completely lost the use of their senses as they have lost their tails.

Dogs should be proud of being canine and live by the high standards of the species. Only thus can we demonstrate our right to a place within a human pack and maintain man's respect. Already such decadence can be seen that it is extremely unlikely that most dogs could survive outside the human pack. It is thus ever more important for

15

the preservation of the super-pack that man continue to find us necessary and to fulfil his role as our provider and pack leader.

The conditions under which many of us live today—however comfortable they may be—are far removed from those of our ancestors. There are many things which we developed in earlier times which are still part of the instinctive behaviour which every young pup receives through his genetic memory, things which do not have an immediately understood relevance to the modern environment of many household dogs. Somehow we must find a way to educate and inform our young to prevent the confusion and psychological problems which can result. Since so few dogs now live under anything resembling natural pack conditions and increasingly may be the only canine in a mixed-species pack, probably living largely in a contained environment and meeting other dogs only on brief exercise and sanitary excursions, an impossible burden is thrown upon nursing bitches to educate and inform their pups during their first few weeks of life. Fortunately, humans are becoming fascinated with their own behaviour patterns and with their much greater problems in controlling and redirecting ancient instincts which conflict with modern standards. To understand themselves they have studied other species, ourselves included, and often have a greater understanding of these matters than does the dog in their pack. The most intelligent of them find ways of showing a young pup the circumstances in which specific instincts are meant to be exercised and devise play situations to compensate for lack of opportunity to fulfil them. Until there is a radical change in the number of literate canines (and I appreciate how few dogs are likely to read these words) it is to humans that we must look for help in maintaining understanding of such things among dogs. For the preservation of those ancient traditions of canine history and law I am less optimistic, if dogs do not overcome the reading block. Race memory can retain much of the emotional core but it requires interpretation. Those fortunate enough to be members of a canine sub-pack within a mixed–species pack have a particular responsibility here, for where humans have tried to understand our laws, morals and beliefs they have often got them wrong.

The fox-hounds, beagles and other hunting packs who still live together in large numbers should form a perfect reservoir for this knowledge, but unfortunately the conditioning imposed by humans in such circumstances does not develop their intellectual interests, and the preservation of canine lore is now largely in the hands of residents in professional breeding kennels and such traditionalists as farm and shepherd dogs.

2 CHOOSING AN OWNER

Most of you will already have owners and your own experience will have told you how difficult it is for any pup to exercise much choice at all. Partly this is because we are all so eager to meet new people and discover more about the world that it is difficult not to find almost any new human interesting; partly it is because someone looking for a dog is probably presenting a rather special image of himself and he may be quite different after living with one of us for some time. Most important is that the onus of choice is on the other paw: it is the human who makes the real decision. But that decision can be influenced.

The human will probably be provided with a whole range of information about parentage, likely inherited characteristics and the way we are expected to grow up. We can only assess the evidence before our eyes. If a family comes to choose then it is likely that they are looking for a family dog, but the fact that a person arrives on his own does not necessarily mean that he will be the sole owner. Smells can help a little, but pups do not have the sophisticated knowledge needed to identify the wide range of human smells, so that their usefulness is more apparent when mother is around to size up the situation and push an individual pup towards a particular owner. Even then it is easy to get things wrong. A smell of babies, especially on a man, is a fairly positive indication of a family home (and on a man it is likely to suggest a warm and loving disposition). Men smelling of women and of female perfume will at first also suggest a paired domestic situation—but you could be

18

wrong. Naturally, other animal scents will help to identify the non–human occupants of a household. Sharing a household with other animals can mean divided attention, but they also offer you friendship—most valuable if your humans are away from home for long stretches of the day.

Voice, the general manner of movement and the way in which humans handle you are probably the best guide to their temperaments—and if the visitor is not looking for a dog for him or herself one must hope that apparently caring people will be equally careful about the home for which they are choosing.

Unfortunately, many humans who should never be allowed to do so decide to keep dogs, and others do not have any idea of what kind of breed is suitable for them. If only we could find out as much about potential owners as humans can about us from our breed and our pedigrees. Of course, humans have interfered so much in our development that the concentration of certain characteristics has been greatly influenced by their needs. We have had no such opportunity, and the longer life-span of the average human being and the lack of any particular 'season' in the human female does make selective breeding for particular aptitudes more difficult for them. Although of a long and noble line myself and capable of carrying off a championship at Crufts or any other gathering in my time, I personally do not support the extremes of specialization. I like to consider myself the complete dog, diverse in interests and adaptable in capabilities. I shall return to this subject later, but for the moment let us look at the more obvious examples of needs linked with particular breed characteristics—needs which are not always appreciated until one is well past puppyhood.

Naturally, large dogs tend to need more space and those with long-ranging legs built for speed and the chase, such as the Afghan, the Saluki and the whole gazehound family, need plenty of room for exercise. Those with tiny legs do not need so much space, nor do they have such stamina (it is a good idea to make it clear to humans from the start

19

that you do not intend to rush to keep up with them if you cannot, nor dawdle when your whole being is dying to feel the wind rushing through your ears), and such dogs may find town living much more pleasant than would their bigger cousins.

Terriers, who have developed a special skill at digging out other animals that have gone to earth, may find it extremely difficult to curb the urge to chase after every rabbit or rodent of which they get the slightest scent. This instinct may be just what the owner wants—and he or she ought to be aware of its characteristic presence, for humans are responsible for it—but be wary for it can also lead to trouble.

Herding breeds may find that they have no occupation with some owners: a working owner may not necessarily smell strongly of sheep or cattle but if a human carries strong city smells, or if his appearance and clothes do not suggest the countryman, the career dog can expect to find little opportunity to exercise professional skills. The frustration can be reduced and some satisfaction gained from taking charge of lesser animals, even in organizing a group of other dogs, but many natural herd dogs will probably have to be content with rounding up the stragglers on family walks and keeping everyone in line. It really is amazing that humans, having nurtured and developed such specialist canine skills over many generations, now seem deliberately to frustrate so many of their dogs.

There may be some tell-tale signs—sporting clothes, mud on the boots and suchlike—to indicate the kind of home on offer, but humans tend to change their clothing for different occupations and remove such evidence as though trying to disguise from those they meet what they have been doing and to camouflage one part of their lives from the rest. While we enjoy a good sniff to pick up all the gossip and share it with most other dogs humans can be extremely secretive. I wonder to what extent they realize how much they give away when we really get to know them?

20

Usually there is no opportunity to set one potential owner against another. You have to make up your mind on the moment—too often dogs have thought that they would wait for something better, only to end up with a much worse bargain. There is a lot of luck involved and both parties have to search out an instant rapport. Then you can make an immediate display to either attract or repel the potential owner.

Set out to produce a definite reaction from which you can begin to make your character assessment to back up what you may already have gleaned about background and environment from physical evidence. Be outgoing, do not hold back. Licks all over the face can often produce a very clear response: sometimes shocked horror (not always a bad sign, but look out for other warnings); sometimes surprised delight (probably a sign of someone in desperate need of affection who will be a devoted owner); and some-times a sloppy sentimental gooiness (a danger sign for it shows the kind of owner who will be over-indulgent to the extent of feeding you all your favourite foods but forget-ting what your health demands, and probably balance this by being extremely inconsiderate whenever anything else upsets them). This last kind of personality often seems to go with fur coats, several strings of pearls and the perfume of Chanel Number Five mingled with a strong odour of gin and tonic. Try nibbling at the coat to test this kind of potential owner's genuine reactions.

Naturally, if you feel instinctively that a particular human who comes to see you is just the owner you are looking for, then do your best to make him, or her, like you. Be friendly, without knocking him over or smother-ing him with dribble: wag your tail and hold his eye with a bright friendly look in yours, or perhaps even try a sad-and-lost look if you think this human is one who will not be able to resist that old gambit.

If you don't like someone, and think it safer to take the risk that nothing better may turn up, it is very easy to put a potential owner off. Growl, snarl, turn your back on any overture and you will almost never be chosen. But take care, make sure that the owner who is passing you on gets plenty of friendly attention when the stranger is not around or you will get a reputation for being an unpleasant dog, which could seriously prejudice your chances of a happy home.

A word of warning, too, if you are the top dog of your litter, or in any way a dominant dog. There is a temptation to choose a weak owner whom you can boss about. Resist it, for in the long run this can only lead to unhappiness and neurosis on both sides, for the human will try to tell you what to do and attempt to become your leader without ever being decisive enough to get you to follow his decisions. Moreover, you will find that the human species are absolutely hopeless at being much more than coat brushers and food preparers if unable to maintain a pack-leader position.

Mother dogs should always try to help in the selection of a first owner for their pups if they get the chance to do so. Not only do they have an experience of humans that their young ones lack, they also know the character of each one of their litter better than anyone else and can most effectively match the two. They should reassure their youngsters as much as possible when they send them off on their own and pass on as much basic knowledge as they can, while not confusing young minds with too much detailed information which may not be relevant in their new situation. The rudiments of self-defence and basic confidences will have been learned in litter play; sensory skills should have been stimulated and developed and danger sensitivities awakened. But simple toilet training is probably the most important for giving the new relationship a good start and it will add to the comfort of both the pup and his new owner. With so many other pressures on a mother's time and energy there are some lessons that will not be fully learned and a pup should be made to understand that he must continue with his studies and make what use he can of human help in learning.

Most of us spend our whole adult lives with one human and mixed-species pack but sometimes death or change of circumstance may mean that we have to choose again. With the experience gained of humans a second choice should be much more skilfully made, but it is surprising how many dogs forget that they are no longer pups and start thinking of a new home full of active youngsters when they might be much better suited to a quieter environment. Getting used to a new batch of noisy brats when one is accustomed to an established régime can be difficult. Humans, too, often fail to realize the advantages of taking on a grown dog. If it has had a good previous home where no vicious or neurotic habits have been developed, an adult dog will cause none of the havoc which some young pups do. Of course, an elderly dog may require a little more care and consideration, but in other ways he will be less demanding.

There are also occasions when a dog may decide on his or her own accord that it is time for a change. If, once launched into the world, you are dissatisfied with your owner, finding a replacement home (and even escaping from the first) may not be easy. It may be necessary to exist for some time without any human support and, although in theory you will have the chance to exercise much greater selectivity, you may find that in some respects you could regret your decision. The dog whose first thought is for creature comforts would be wiser to think again and yet again before planning to look for something new.

If you are allowed a fairly free-ranging life it is unlikely that you will find a situation otherwise so oppressive that you must make a deliberate flight from it before you can even begin to look for another—and it could be that all territories within reasonable reach are already occupied. Brief absences, if they can be arranged, will allow the dissatisfied to prospect personalities, affluence (garbage is often a useful indicator, although many more affluent homes now have machines which treat their surplus food and send it down the drains), comfort rating and other animal competition. A social call to see how one is treated is always wise.

Relocation involves a high element of risk, for humans often have as strong a respect for other people's property as we ourselves have for territory and, however much they may like you, they may feel bound to return you to the original home—it is often part of their law to do so, especially if you are carrying an identification disc. Losing your disc helps foil identification if you are sufficiently far from territory where you might be recognized, but this can also bring dangers: a dog without an owner is not protected from persecution by those genocidal humans who seek to remove us from what they consider is their world. In towns especially a dog may risk being classed a stray and rounded up; often they are never heard of again.

3 THE NEW PACK

So the die has been thrown and the decision made regarding your new territory and your new pack. You may feel powerless and full of trepidation or you may be bouncing with cheery optimism at what your human seems to promise: but whoever you find yourself being taken off by do *not* panic; play it cool and leave it for the humans to reveal themselves. If you like, play up the 'little dog lost' to ensure that you get lots of attention and start off in your new home with your owner falling over him or herself to make you happy—it makes it much more difficult for them to start being tough later.

A pup should never waste time mourning the separation from its mother and its siblings. Mum would probably have kicked you out soon enough and the competition with your brothers and sisters could only have got more intense. Preserve your energy to cope with the problems of your new environment.

For most youngsters this will be their first real journey, and it can often be a disturbing experience if you do not know what to expect. You will probably be put into a basket, unless more than one human has come to collect you and they think that they can manage to carry you in their arms. Actually, a basket or a box is very much better, much though you might like the idea of those arms around you, for then you can have your own small environment, an area of privacy and safety around you. You will probably be taken in a car—a box moving on wheels—and, if you have not yet travelled in one, you must expect a

25

certain amount of bumping motion as you travel. This does you no harm and anything you may have heard about it making you ill is nonsense. Dogs who bring up their food when travelling are suffering from nervousness, not motion—at least in my opinion. If you decide you are going to be sick then of course you will be, but it is only the very rare dog that is travel-sick for physiological reasons. Because so many dogs get foolishly nervous some humans think it best to give a mild tranquillizer or a stomach-settling pill before embarking on a journey and, if you are given a tablet before leaving, you can reasonably expect that this is what it is for and should offer no resistance to taking it. (There will be a discussion of medication-taking later.)

If your journey is a long one you may well have a halt to have some food and water and a chance to relieve yourself. I know that small pups feel the need to respond to sudden urges to defecate or pass urine but it will make a much better impression if you can hold on to it until such an opportunity. If you are in a cardboard or solid box lined with plenty of newspaper it is a sign that your new human realizes the problem and if you have to do it in the box the human will realize that it is even more unpleasant for you than it is for him or her. If you are travelling in a public vehicle, like a train which cannot stop to suit your human and yourself, you may be offered sheets of newspaper to relieve yourself on.

At the end of your journey and before you go indoors attempt to relieve yourself again. Experienced humans will give you the opportunity to do so. If you find yourself taken straight indoors then an attempt to return to the door, accompanied by a soft whine, will give the owner an idea of your needs and probably please him tremendously as well. Of course, many pups are so nervous that they simply cannot restrain themselves and on such a frightening and exciting occasion any reasonable human will forgive them.

Knowledgeable owners will help you to establish a toilet

pattern, carefully watching for those signs of your increasing discomfort and then carrying you outside or to whatever toilet place has been planned, and always providing an opportunity to relieve yourself a short time after meals, when a dog is usually most in need. No dog wants to soil his sleeping area but remember that for humans the sleeping area covers the whole house—and for some strange reason they have laws which frequently extend it to other places such as pavements, too. Very young puppies probably will not be able to hold out all night without at least urinating but they should not get in too much of a state about it. If humans do not arrange an indoor toilet area or some way of getting out they cannot blame you for it; however, do try to choose somewhere that can be cleaned up easily afterwards.

Owners will probably have prepared a proper sleeping place for you; inspect it carefully to see that it is situated out of draughts and is comfortable (even the best intentioned humans sometimes forget there may be draughts at floor level that they can't feel when they are standing up). A comfortable sleeping place is very important, especially for the very young who need a lot of restful sleep. A basket or a box with a warm blanket in it will probably be provided: try them out. If you do not like their position make that clear by going and lying down somewhere else which you find better—but make sure that you are noticed. Your choice may prove inconvenient for the rest of the household so you must be prepared for an element of compromise. If the bedding is unsatisfactory you can try pulling it about and looking for something more appropriate—but do be sensible: only the youngest pups are likely to get away with stealing any cushion they like without being severely punished. Often a position a few inches off the floor will avoid the worst of the draughts. Some dog beds are set on feet to achieve this. If you are of a small breed and know that you will not soon outgrow it, you might make a claim for the seat of a comfortable chair.

Human homes differ considerably in size, scale, the way

27

in which they are partitioned and the facilities they offer. Among humans and their mixed packs there seems to be no accepted pattern of territorial rights; these are arrived at as a precarious balance within the household and are often changeable, although it would be wise for a new arrival to follow the human guide-lines at the start. The fewer people and animals in the pack the less conflict is likely to occur, but reduced numbers can mean boredom and loneliness for those left without play partners or deserted for long parts of the day while the humans are, as they say, 'at work'. The humans will attempt to decide the overall apportioning of territory and may seek to exclude you from large parts which they control, leaving only a shared area in which your personal territory is restricted to your bed, although even this may be challenged by some pack members (especially felines). By the way, be prepared to find some odd companions. Creatures which both canine and breed instinct may recognize as enemies or prey may be co-members of the pack and you will be expected to accept them as such. Sometimes this is a requirement it proves impossible to meet when some surprise action triggers off ancient mechanisms, bringing great shame upon us. Always remember, pack before prey—for you will not, except in the most extreme circumstances, be expected to demonstrate your natural reaction for outsiders.

On first arrival your human may confine you to a very small territory or you may be encouraged to investigate the whole house. A timid pup may find it easier to cope with a small environment which he can check out and feel safe in, perhaps retreating into the box or basket in which he travelled until he has gained confidence. A more adventurous dog may wish to explore straight away.

Once bladder and bowels are comfortable begin to explore, first with the nose and eyes and then investigating further. Humans may not let you beyond the door. Some, usually those who are planning to offer a working partnership (with you the junior partner of course—and no chance

28

of changing the situation, for humans prove useless at role reversal in such cases: they are physically equipped for certain tasks, we for others, and their role happens to be the controlling one), expect you to stay in the kitchen or even in some building outside the house. You may have a cage or kennel as a restricted and very private territory which enables you to have a rather larger unshared area outside the house than is possible inside. These conditions usually guarantee a pretty active life but might prove a strain upon a more sentimental kind of dog. Fortunately, owners who offer such a set-up normally take great care to pair themselves with a dog of just the kind that this life suits best.

On your tour of inspection be prepared to meet absolutely anything. Small humans, felines, other canines, changes of surface and temperature, humidity, vegetation, machinery and noise, are all likely to be encountered, and you should approach all calmly, quietly and slowly. This gives you protection from any sudden change which could lead to injury and will lessen the threat which you may present to existing pack members. If you should meet hostility do not attack (unless it is a creature trying to attack your human): offer appeasement presentations and be ready to retreat if they are not accepted. Later, when you have gained acceptance and have got to know your pack mates' weaknesses and strengths, you may press for a bigger share of pack resources, but at first respect the claims of those there before you.

You will probably find that certain parts of the house are forbidden to you. They will not be the same in all cases for they will depend upon the attitudes of the humans, the other pack members and the contents of the rooms. Some humans like you to share their sleeping arrangements, some are horrified at the idea; some have many fragile objects on low tables which may easily be knocked over by an energetically wagging tail. A considerate owner will probably let you have a complete tour of the house in your early settling-in period so that you are not tantalized with longings to find out what lies behind each door, but they will also make it quite clear from the start which rooms, or pieces of furniture, etc., are to be considered 'out-of-bounds'.

Unfortunately, humans are not always consistent and may permit you to sit on a sofa one day but not the next. If they realized how confusing it can be when they complain about actions of ours which they have happily accepted on an earlier occasion they might try harder to establish a single set of rules that both sides know and respect. You may also find that things permitted as a pup are no longer tolerated as you become adult. Of course, the charm of the very young does tend to let them get away with anything, but if humans could establish a suitable social contract from the beginning of their relationship with us, and keep to it, a great deal of frustration and unhappiness could be prevented.

When you have done your initial reconnaissance and ensured that no danger lurks you can get down to having some food, for you are bound to be hungry. Even the most stupid human seems to realize that providing a suitable meal and a good bowl of clean water as soon as you arrive is a basic task. Don't try to eat until you have fully satisfied yourself about your surroundings and calmed any nagging fears—you do not want to give yourself indigestion. And do not gulp the food down. Your human will probably have discovered from your previous owner what kind of diet you have had and the frequency of meals, and at first will serve you what you are used to and at similar times. However, this is not always the case, so be prepared for something you are not used to eating. If you are going to establish some idea of your standards of *haute cuisine* do not betray yourself by eating anything and everything just because you are ravenous. Take a good drink of water, too. And do not forget to give the human sufficient warning when you want to go out to perform the inevitable result. I suppose it is no use reminding puppies that they have only small insides and that they should not stuff themselves but eat rather less more often—better for older dogs, too, although few of us learn it until we end up with stomach problems, flatulence and wind.

You will be emotionally, if not actually physically, tired and should rest as soon as possible, even though it is not the humans' sleeping time. If they are making for their beds they may encourage you to follow them, or you may find other animals in the pack would welcome the warmth of a bed companion, but you may simply be locked up in your own core territory. Of course, you will feel lonely and you will suddenly realize that you have not got mother or brothers or sisters with you. A few tears won't do you any harm, and might even make you feel better, but persistent wailing will only annoy the humans. Sometimes, if they are sentimental, they may come down to comfort you. But don't think that that can go on for long: humans rapidly get bored by anything which places demands upon them. Humans who have wide experience with dogs will ignore you anyway, for they will be aware that if they give in this time you will expect to get your own way again (such level-headed humans probably are just as hard on their own litters).

When you wake next morning try to repress the urge to bark out the news to everybody. They may want to sleep for a good time longer than you do. After a few days you will soon get an idea of the humans' daily timetable (remember that they change their behaviour pattern for a day or two in every seven days, perhaps getting up much later or staying up much later). Eventually, you may discover that the humans like to be awakened by you, but make very certain that that is indeed what they want before you offer your services.

4 A SENSIBLE DIET

Are you a gourmet or a glutton? It is amazing how faddy some dogs can become about their food, and how stupid others can be in stuffing anything and everything that comes their way straight down their throats. Have you ever taken a good look at your teeth, or thought about the way in which your digestive system works? Probably not—most dogs are too busy thinking about the food itself—but teeth do tell us quite a lot about the kind of diet which they have developed to deal with. The shape and placing of our teeth clearly indicate that they were originally designed for biting and tearing meat and not for chewing plants. We are carnivorous and eat other animals, which our ancestors had to hunt and catch unless they were lucky enough to come across one freshly dead. Living with man has led to many changes and modifications so that now we can be almost as omnivorous as the humans themselves, provided that our diet is well-balanced. But our physique was developed to make us efficient and successful hunters and our stomachs were able to expand to cope with a large meal after a kill, or to contract during a long period of fasting when prey was scarce. That is why we 'wolf' (the verb is most appropriate) down as much as we can when we get the opportunity—a racial memory from the time when it was the practical thing to do.

Today, few of us have to hunt or scavenge for our food. Our humans have been trained to obtain and prepare it for us. They are extremely interested in food and have studied diet extremely carefully, for they are much more particular about what they eat than we tend to be. Perhaps it is because so many of their other senses have largely atrophied that they have concentrated on developing that of taste. Perhaps it is because they have made eating into such an elaborate pack ritual. Not only have they devised ways of preparing and elaborating food to stimulate their taste sense, they have also scientifically studied the composition of the various kinds of edible material and worked out what proportions of these constituents are needed to keep a body healthy—and they have done this not only for themselves but also for us, and for some other animals, too, while they were about it. They have discovered that some foods contain substances called vitamins, some of which are absolutely necessary to our health (although different ones are necessary for different animals), and that various minerals, proteins and carbohydrates are necessary for growth, energy and fitness. Our digestive systems, for instance, can cope efficiently with sugars and cooked starch, and the mixture of food which the omnivorous humans eat can also suit us well. We have the advantage over our feline relations in that we can manufacture Vitamin A from carrots, tomatoes and some other types of vegetables. Furthermore, we can create Vitamin C in our own bodies so that we do not need it in our diet.

Over the thousands of years before we set up our symbiotic partnership with man we learned from hard experience what was the best food for a dog, what herbs made useful medicines, what meats produced best milk in our bitches. But since the beginning of the man-dog time we have become less dependent on our own resources and although our hereditary knowledge still guides us on these things it is not perhaps as exact as it was. Indeed, for many of us access to suitable animal or herbal sources is impossible. We must be grateful, therefore, for the work that humans have put in on our behalf. The 'nutritionists' (for that is what they are called) who have carried out the research, have formulated all kinds of foods which are

33

pre-prepared, and which humans can buy in canned or dried form, making it possible to have food always readily available.

Some of these preparations are quite tasty and many provide a balanced diet, if used according to the manufacturers' instructions—and often a much better one than would be possible if it were left to you and your owner to find the individual ingredients. Most canned food is a mixture of meat, cereals, vitamins and minerals—but some of the more expensive brands contain no cereal and these should be supplemented with dog biscuits. If your human buys the expensive kinds it is almost certain that biscuits will be made available too, even if the human is not aware of the dietary need. Biscuits may themselves contain vitamin and mineral supplements and they are also good for the teeth as well as helping to provide both energy and bulk to keep you regular and your motions solid.

As well as canned food, humans may obtain processed food which may be presented as semi-moist pellets or in crunchy dry pieces. Some of these are extremely palatable. Naturally, if your food is very dry, you will probably want to drink a lot more water. Insist that your humans provide it.

One thing that these pre-prepared foods never supply is a good bone to gnaw on. Not only is a bone a satisfying possession and a pleasant toy, it is actually good for the teeth. Fortunately, humans have learned that this is one of the things that they are expected to provide and even when they rarely offer fresh meat they will usually acquire a bone for us. If you find that they have been stripping one that has an interesting shape or smell then do not hesitate to demand it: you will rarely be refused, although you may be expected to leave it behind when you visit certain parts of the humans' territory. Try to avoid cooked ribs or other splintery bits. They may cause a terrible stomach ache and need an operation by the vet to remove them. They can be fatal. Artificial 'bones' are sometimes provided by squeamish owners who object to the real thing; they are not a satisfactory substitute.

Our ancestors, who relied upon killing their own meat, had access to the whole carcass and could choose any bones they liked as well as obtaining additional nutrients from the partially digested stomach contents of their prey. The full range of vitamins and minerals is not presented in the chopped-up pieces of butcher's meat which humans buy for us; it must therefore be obtained from vegetables or from proprietary preparations if we are lucky enough to eat largely fresh meat instead of laboratory-prepared foods. Do not, therefore, reject those meal-time left-overs from the humans' dinner table, and keep an eye open out-of-doors for access to grass and other herbs which could be beneficial. Milk, cheese, fish and eggs are all full of protein, while offal meats—liver and entrails—are also very nutritious. However, never eat liver when you are suffering from looseness or diarrhoea as it will only make it worse (on the other hand, it is worth eating liver whenever you can get it if you are prone to constipation). Uncooked white of egg and uncooked fish should be avoided because they contain anti-vitamin factors.

Some dogs always like to have their meat raw, perhaps because they think that is a more natural way of taking food, but in domestic conditions this is not wise for the animal will not be fresh. Some humans consider that meat should always be cooked because this will destroy any harmful parasites and bacteria which may be present and it is certainly a wise precaution. If you prefer to take the risk and eat it raw you should still refuse it if it comes straight from the refrigerator for that may result in your catching a chill—and you should ignore it if it has been around too long. It is never worth taking the risk, however much it means fighting against the instinct to eat whatever you can, for even cooked meat can harbour disease if it is left out for many hours. However, provided it is fresh there is no need to be fussy about the kind of meat. Refuse fish unless the bones have already been removed—or ground—

35

as they can cause considerable discomfort if they get stuck in your throat. Chicken bones and others which are needle-like—and all cooked bones which become splintery—should be avoided if possible, although smooth small bones which pass through the digestive system will be dissolved by the acid in the stomach and add useful calcium to the diet. Wise humans will not offer dangerous bones, nor will they leave food down in your eating place if there is more than you can eat at any one meal-time.

Humans will offer you food every few hours when you are very young but as you grow up they will cut down the number of meal-times and increase the quantity at each. When you eat is largely controlled by when the food is provided. Most dogs in healthy condition can be happy with one good meal a day but some of the larger breeds (the bloodhounds and boxers, for example) have gastric problems if the stomach is overloaded and will be happier if fed twice daily. Provided that we are not overfed, two meals a day is probably more enjoyable for all of us. If your owner offers you only one meal and you can resist eating all of it and then demand a fresh meal at the opposite end of the day you may be able to convince him that you know best, but leaving food is more than most of us can manage unless it is unwholesome.

Should you be offered food which you feel you can under no circumstances stomach, or which you think is less than healthy, make sure that your human sees that you are leaving it: do not just refuse it or he may think that you are simply off-colour and suffering from a momentary loss of appetite. You might bark or whine to attract his attention and then show your disapproval by turning away from the food, perhaps even deliberately turning it over.

What humans do not realize is that smaller breeds, despite their size, often need a proportionally greater amount of food. If you get a single morning meal this may help you to avoid trips out for toilet purposes at night but if you are a working dog try to insist that your main meal comes in the evening and that you have something light, a few biscuits perhaps, in the morning of a heavy working day. I personally like to have a main meal of meat with cereal and then a second light meal of biscuit with a bowl of milk—and water, of course, for whenever I get thirsty during day or night. Most important is to be punctual at meal-times—and that means being much more punctual than your owner, for humans are not nearly as well organized to match the natural clock as we are. They become dependent upon all kinds of clocks and alarms—or upon us—to get them up and tell them when it is time for what. Regular timing is vital for a comfortable digestive system and to keep toilet outings regular—do not let humans forget it.

I include tables (pp. 39–41), worked out by a human scientist to show our nutritional needs, the value of various foods, and examples of healthy diets. If you are being encouraged to eat greater quantities than suggested, you will probably have obesity problems and all the side-effects which they can produce. You would think that the frequency with which humans talk about slimming and their middle-age spread would make them much more sensitive to what they do to us, but it doesn't seem to make them any more sensible about themselves or us. There are many other unlisted foods to which individuals take a particular liking. If you discover that you enjoy, say, grapes or chocolate or currant buns, there is no harm in eating them in moderation, although very sweet things can seriously damage your teeth if taken to excess. Humans try to counter their weakness for such things by brushing their teeth with bristles and still end up having to have them removed and artificial ones inserted. Although I have often been given such sweets none of my owners has ever offered to brush my teeth and counter the decay they cause.

If you take a fancy to a particular food it would be sensible to let your humans see how much you enjoy it: then they will probably make it a frequent extra, particularly if it is something which is rather unusual for dogs to eat. Humans love to say that they have something other humans do not have, and this ranges not only from an expensive car to a rare disease but includes a proprietary claim for any idiosyncrasies that you exhibit. A simple trick, occasionally helping the cat to wash, liking Chinese cooking or preferring a particular brew of ale—anything will do. But, if you find your human bragging about you, do not let them down: you must be ready to show off your 'speciality' before friends and acquaintances even if it is the last thing in your head—otherwise the human may lose face and be embarrassed. Put on a good performance and exaggerate everything, for men and women rarely have the sensory capacity to notice anything done with subtlety.

Be very wary of accepting any of your favourite treats from strangers. They could be drugged. Growl at the profferer, even if your human is there, and then they will probably give the present to your human. This will give you the chance to assess the relationship between them on an instinctive level. Encourage your owner to pass on the treat if you feel all is well, or continue to growl as a warning to him of the basic unfriendliness behind the other's apparent warmth if that is what you detect.

NUTRITIVE VALUE OF SOME DOG FOODS

Food	Energy Cal/lb	Protein %	Vitamins A	Vitamins B group	Calcium	Roughage
Lean beef	550	20	—	**	—	—
Ox liver	500	17	***	***	—	—
Ox heart	500	19	—	**	—	—
Ox lung	500		—	*	—	—
Ox tripe (dressed)	450	15	—	*	*	—
Shank bone (raw)	300	15	—	*	***	—
Carrots	100	1	*	*	*	**
Potatoes, mashed	500	1	—	*	—	**
Brown bread	1,000	9	—	*	*	**
Biscuits and meals	1,600	10	*	**	**	**
Canned, meaty	400	10	**	**	**	—
Canned, with cereal	500	8	**	**	**	*
'Soft moist'	1,300	20	**	**	**	**
Balanced dog meal	1,500	24	**	**	**	**

* = useful contribution
** = adequate amount
*** = more than adequate

DAILY ENERGY REQUIREMENTS FOR ADULT HOUSEDOGS

Approximate Weight		Representative Breeds	Calories per day
lb	kg		
2	0.9	Chihuahua	150
5	2.2	Maltese terrier, Yorkshire terrier	250
8	3.6	miniature dachshund, toy poodle	350
10	4.5	papillon, Pekinese	400
15	6.8	Cairn terrier, miniature poodle, Shetland sheep-dog	550
20	9.1	corgi, dachshund, fox terrier, whippet	700
25	11.3	cocker spaniel, Irish terrier	800
30	13.6	beagle, Kerry Blue, schnauzer	900
40	18.1	bull terrier, English springer spaniel	1100
50	22.6	Airedale, bulldog, chow chow	1300
60	27.2	boxer, greyhound, retrievers, setters	1500
80	36.3	Alsatian (German shepherd), Rhodesian ridgeback	1800
100	40.8	bloodhound, bullmastiff, Pyrenean	2300
150	63.5	Great Dane, mastiff, Newfoundland	3200
200	90.7	St Bernard	4000

Notes:
1 This chart is only a guide. There is, as with humans, a great deal of individual variation in total food (energy) requirement.
2 If the dog is not obese, weight is a more useful guide to food needs than breed, so for crossbreds judge requirement by their weight.
3 If the dog appears to be losing weight, although eating plenty, consult the vet; if gaining weight, severely reduce the amount of food until the correct weight is regained.
4 Puppies need much more food. As a very broad rule-of-thumb, puppies need about twice as much food as an adult dog of the same weight. For example, a 30lb (13.6kg) Labrador pup needs about twice as much food as a 30lb (13.6kg) beagle. From about ten weeks of age, puppies eat more than they will need as adults. The peak is reached at about six months. After that age food must be reduced or the dog will become obese.
5 Puppies can be reared on the same balanced diets as are suitable for adult dogs, if the food is not too hard or lumpy.

SOME ALTERNATIVE WELL-BALANCED DIETS FOR ADULT HOUSEDOGS

Small dog Weight 10lb (4.5kg) Calories/day 400	Average size dog Weight 35lb (16kg) Calories/day 1,000	Large dog Weight 65lb (30kg) Calories/day 1,600

Morning meal
¼pt (140g) whole cow's milk
2oz (56g) brown bread
Afternoon meal
¼lb (113g) minced lean beef
  or heart or chicken
1oz (28g) grated carrot
1 or 2 small dog biscuits
	Main meal
	12oz (340g) dressed ox tripe
	4oz (170g) plain dog meal
	½oz (14g) sterilized bone flour
	Supplementary meal
	8 small dog biscuits
	Saucer (50g) cow's milk
	5 drops cod-liver oil
		4oz (113g) ox liver
		12oz (340g) ox tripe
		12oz (340g) plain dog meal
		1oz (28g) sterilized bone flour
		1 large dog biscuit
		(*Note:* Divide between two meals
		  if preferred)

Morning meal
¼lb (140g) minced beef
2oz (56g) puppy meal
Afternoon meal
2–3 small dog biscuits
Saucer (50g) cow's milk
	7oz (198g) canned dog food
	7oz (198g) proprietary dog meal
	8 small or 2 large dog biscuits
	(*Note:* Divide between two meals
	  if preferred)
		15oz (425g) canned dog food
		12oz (340g) proprietary dog meal
		1 large dog biscuit
		(*Note:* Divide between two meals
		  if preferred)

Morning meal
4oz (113g) canned dog food
2oz (56g) puppy meal
Afternoon meal
4–5 small dog biscuits
	10oz (283g) complete dog meal
	3oz (84g) canned dog meat
	(*Note:* Divide between two meals
	  if preferred)
		16oz (454g) complete dog meal
		4oz (113g) canned dog food
		(*Note:* Divide between two meals
		  if preferred)

Note: Find a diet which suits your dog and stick to it. Sudden changes of diet can cause upset digestion. Fresh drinking water should always be available.

5 SENSE ABOUT SEX

There is no denying that one of the strongest of all the instinctive drives possessed by living creatures is that to reproduce themselves. Only thus can they perpetuate themselves and their species. In most animals, including ourselves, this is brought about by the attraction of one sex for the other and their conjunction to produce young— or so used to be the case, for humans have recently developed means by which offspring can be produced without sire or dam ever having met. On rare occasions they apply this method to themselves, often use it with farm animals and occasionally apply this 'artificial insemination' to ourselves when a particularly fine dog cannot easily be transported on a personal visit to court a selected mate.

Such means, however, have no effect on the instinctive drive to couple with a partner of the opposite sex. Our bodies are patterned to obey the natural order but, natural though this urge may be, it may run counter to the way the humans want to run the world.

Today, all thinking species are being forced to reconsider the endless mating and multiplication of the world's millions. Once the competitive conditions of the natural environment kept a balance between populations and resources. It was a hard world, but not an overcrowded one. The artificial circumstances of today have interfered with the natural cycles of abundance and barrenness. Man has struggled to find protection from the predation, disease and natural disasters that used to control the increase in numbers. He has changed not only his own survival rate but that of almost every other animal on earth. His agriculture, hunting, industry, mining and other forms of exploitation have destroyed entire species and eaten up areas which provided food and shelter for others, forcing them towards extinction or into different territories where, in turn, they overbalance the environment. So far has this been carried that humans themselves have begun to form groups devoted to the protection and re-establishment of endangered species.

For those animals, such as the cats and ourselves, who have joined man's domestic pack the conditions of our way of life protect us from the natural dangers and offer us instead a whole range of medical and other aids to increase our survival. Some species, the horse for instance, would no longer exist were it not for man's need of it (and, when humans turned to the steam-engine and then the motorcar for transport, horse numbers were rapidly reduced to only a fraction of those kept formerly). We dogs could perhaps have suffered a similar fate, being hunted like our wolf relations or the early horses. Fortunately, we showed how useful we could be to man; he has never found a way to create a robot or an electronic device which can fully take our place. When the anti-canine publicity machine is broadcasting its charges that we pollute the city streets, spread disease and consume food needed by the starving humans of the world I sometimes wonder what may yet be in store for us.

What is certain is that if each of us was to be able freely to follow through our very natural urges there would soon be so many dogs in the world that we might have to do something about the problem ourselves. Humans have to face up to an overpopulation problem already. Their numbers have, in most countries, grown far beyond their natural levels. They have been forced to develop means to deal with the situation and it is to them that we must look for the solution of our problem.

Some of my readers may be shocked at what I have to say. Others may feel that my proposals are all very well for

43

an old dog such as I, who has already had his share of fun and thrills, but very hard upon the younger generation. To them I can only answer that we have to make the best of the situation and I believe that the individual must be prepared to sacrifice some of his liberties for the greater good. The only alternative is to attempt to put the clock back and return to our way of life before we teamed up with man—and frankly the chances of that succeeding are as remote as those of some of our idealistic humans who think that prayers and home-made bread can bring about a new ideal society.

For some animals there are only certain seasons of the year when they feel the urge to mate, and most females have only one period each year when they are prepared to accept a male. For humans the situation is exactly the opposite. As you may have noticed when accompanying them, humans seem eager to perform everywhere and anywhere, a habit which has been responsible for their rapid increase despite the way in which they periodically fight each other to reduce their numbers.

In our own case, life with man has changed us from our natural condition: wild canine females come into oestrus (are ready to be fertilized) and feel receptive to males only once each year and males are only seasonally fertile. They also take from one to two years to reach sexual maturity. We modern dogs are sexually adult at six months old; our females may present themselves in oestrus twice a year and our males are always ready. Some young bitches may appear to have three seasons, but the first is usually false; some breeds, such as the basenjis, still have only one each year.

If every dog were free to seek out every bitch he wanted and every bitch were permitted to conceive whenever she was in season the number of puppies which would result would soon bring the canine population to unmanageable proportions. All animals (and man himself, as he would readily admit) have developed a breeding pattern which is designed to keep up the appropriate population for the

44

resources of the terrain and the likely survival rate when faced with natural dangers. But we do not live in a natural habitat and the dangers to which we are exposed are not natural ones. An extremely skilled medical service helps us to recover from all but the most virulent diseases and most terrible accidents. Something has to be done to correct the imbalance.

'Instinct is right!' I can hear you cry, and I understand your feelings. But consider how much you have learned the wisdom of overriding instinct in other areas to make your domestic life more satisfactory. However, celibacy and restraint are more than most of us can sustain and so the onus for population control passes to our humans. We must not feel too resentful, therefore, at being kept indoors at the time that we feel the need to fulfil our procreative urges, or when called to heel and held hard on the leash when opportunity presents itself outdoors.

I believe that most human beings understand the difficulties we have in such situations and, although they will be firm, will have sympathy for the struggle that goes on inside us. They are, however, much less tolerant of those dogs which, thwarted of access to a bitch, thrust themselves upon a human. Personally, I do not blame them.

We dogs are not the only animals to encounter these problems. Cats, too, would have a catastrophic population explosion were not restraints applied. Such restraints— I refer, of course, to surgical forms of birth control—are imposed far more frequently on cats than on dogs but I have often wondered why this is so. A bitch who has difficulty in carrying through a conception or for any genetic reason is not likely to produce healthy puppies, or one whose humans are not prepared to accept the responsibility of caring for more puppies, would find life much easier if she were given an hysterectomy or a lesser operation which would also prevent conception. Male dogs can be neutered, as are male cats; this not only removes the possibility of their fertilizing females but removes most of the instinct to copulate (provided that the operation is performed before such habits have become ingrained). It would make life easier for both many humans and many dogs: there are numerous better ways of enjoying life than frustratedly pining for a female. Humans also give themselves an operation called vasectomy which does not impair the male sex drive but makes it impossible for them to reproduce: this could be a way of solving the population problem for our species without altering instinctive behaviour. However, since it is our behaviour that upsets most humans even more that the potential population explosion I doubt whether it will ever become very fashionable.

Humans have also developed forms of medication which can suppress the strong scent signals of the receptive female and drugs for the human female to prevent conception altogether. Similar preparations are available for bitches, and these seem successful.

If humans do not help us to handle our sexual problems in one of these suggested ways they can hardly blame us if we do our best to follow our instincts; I have a great deal of sympathy for the dog who can no longer restrain his need. Having indulged in so much preaching, I make no pretence to have led a celibate youth. It is only fair that I pass on my experience in this.

Unless you are allowed to roam quite freely, as few of us are today (and just as well with the irresponsible drivers and other hazards to be faced), getting out on your own is largely a matter of giving your humans the slip. Bitches will have only to find a way outside the door; their neighbourhood dogs will do the rest if they can gain their liberty. Dogs must find a receptive bitch.

Getting out is largely a matter of watchfulness and taking the opportunity, when it comes, to dive through an open door. It is wise to take up a position surreptitiously prior to some time when you expect the door to be opened: in a hallway at the usual hour for someone's return, for example, or when a delivery man usually calls. Make yourself as unobtrusive as possible and keep quite still so that you are not noticed when the door is opened, and then streak through the gap, or be ready to dash through the moment you hear a key being put in the lock. Do not, however, expect your humans to be pleased by this behaviour. You will have to put up with their disapproval and probably risk punishment and the almost certain limitation of your freedom of movement later. A more cunning move, perhaps, is to rush outside in greeting, bound around a bit and somehow contrive to get locked out. The humans are at fault and if you hide discreetly out of sight before streaking off they probably won't realize what you are up to.

If you do find yourself a mate, you may still have to suffer human interference and may even be subjected to the indignity of having a bucket of water thrown over you just as you have reached a crucial stage in your relationship.

It is not only undignified, it can also be very painful!

Personally I do not think it is worth it and would volunteer for the operation.

Sex is very overrated. There are plenty of other sensual pleasures to enjoy instead and most of those others our humans are only too happy to indulge.

Naturally, it wouldn't do for every dog to follow my advice—but that will never happen, not only because so many of you will remain unconvinced by my arguments but also because humans would not permit it. They need us, and even if they did not there is money to be made from breeding pedigree dogs. Pedigree dogs may get more opportunity for sexual satisfaction than their mongrel relations. This is because most humans place high value on pure breeding and can be very snobbish about pedigrees.

It is true that both mongrel and pedigree bitches can sometimes be very choosy about which mates they will select, but I have always understood this to be on the basis of individual personality rather than on family origin. Naturally, some of us are more attracted to certain physiques and colours, or a variation in scent may play a major part, but I have never met a dog with a race or class prejudice—at least as far as canines of the opposite sex are concerned.

I have been pleased to see the efforts made by humans to remove such prejudices among themselves and, although I would be as sorry to see the blonde beauty of Scandinavia or the elegant blackness of the Ethiopian disappear from the human breeds as I would to see a world without the Afghan or the Labrador, there are some very beautiful and talented humans—such as Miss Cleo Laine—to show that mongrels can be as fine as any known pure-bred. It is strange that, at a time when humans are adopting a more sensible attitude about themselves, they are becoming increasingly biased towards pedigree breeds. This is something that I do not pretend to understand nor can attempt to explain, although I suspect that it has something to do with the sheer financial value attached to a pedigree which is considered an investment. This is something that humans are often concerned with and which they apply to all kinds of things from the way they spend their time, to old pieces of chipped china and the metal collars and leashes they wear around their necks.

Did you realize that, when a pedigree dog mates with a female, his human is often paid money by the owner of the bitch? Talk about easy cash! While I have been preaching restraint there are humans countering with financial inducements—except that it is not the dog that gets the money, although he will probably be treated well to make sure that he is kept in the best of health and always 'performance ready'.

When humans plan such a mating they spend a great deal of time studying their bitch's family tree and that of potential mates before they decide to introduce her to a particular dog. The idea is to match the pair so that any features that are not quite perfect in conforming to their Kennel Club 'breed standard' in the female are corrected by the good qualities of the male. This leads to a genetic balance in the puppies which is more likely to achieve their ideals.

48

6 TRAINING YOUR OWNER

Contrary to a great deal of popular opinion, most human beings have a high level of intelligence, a retentive memory and are adept at problem-solving. Their individual aptitudes vary as widely as our own—in fact, rather more so when you consider how much more alike they are in physical appearance when compared to the variety of canine breeds—but they are all capable of a sophisticated level of training. Because of their intelligence humans will put a great deal of effort into developing a mutual understanding, but you must allow for the considerable differences between their species and ours and remember the basis upon which our relationship with them has developed.

In many ways humans lack our degree of sensual awareness and therefore do not notice many things which are as large as a lamp-post in the canine mind. They have a longer life-span, and therefore tend to be much more aware of past and future than we are. They communicate by a set of sounds which carry meaning from the order in which they are placed, and which vary from territory to territory so that some humans find difficulty in communicating with others according to where they come from— if they have been reared in a different country and have not undergone a special form of training. The humans have devised also a set of marks upon paper which they use to represent these sounds and which you may often see them concentrating upon. In these two ways they have developed their ears and eyes to a higher level of interpretation than ourselves, but in doing so they have lost the ability to gather much of the information which we continually do both from these and our other senses.

Most dogs are able to interpret at least part of the vocabulary (voice meanings) of the humans, and some of us have learned to recognize some of the pattern of marks which they use to record them upon paper so that humans at a different time and in a different place can understand their messages, but it would endanger our other faculties if we ourselves developed these skills very far. Fortunately, most humans are able to understand a similar amount of our visual and vocal communication and recognize our communicatory behaviour. The longer the relationship between a particular dog and a particular human lasts, the more detailed becomes their understanding of each other and a whole repertoire of communication may be developed which is particular to them because of the accidental linking of some gesture or sound with a meaning.

Humans do not have a visible tail, and very few can move their ears, as can our older breeds with upright ears, but nevertheless it is possible to tell quite a lot about their general mood from their posture and their vocal tone. Their whole body stance is an indication of their mood, despite the fact that they will often consciously attempt to obscure depression or anxiety by trying to impose an upright air of confidence. There is no drooping or dragging of the tail—as we do in an attempt to mask our personal scent when we want to avoid attracting attention— but there is a drooping of the shoulders and of all the limbs when the human is depressed. If the shoulders are well squared back, a little too well, look out for that sudden loosening of the control of mind over matter when the body sags and reveals itself. There is a very big difference between this depression and the easy relaxation of the limbs when a human is quietly happy. But if you have any doubts take a close look at the set of the mouth, the edges of which and the tightness of the lips almost always emphasizes the mood. For further confirmation, use your nose. Humans do not seem to have such efficient specialized scent glands as ourselves, but they do perspire all over, although more freely in certain places. Even in sexual matters most humans do not appreciate, or even properly understand, their own smells, and it is only a limited number that take pleasure in them. Instead, they will rub upon their bodies the scents of other animals and of flowers, woods and chemical mixtures which can sometimes be of an overpowering intensity, but which appear both to give them confidence, as though the artificial marking odour were claiming a territory around them, and to act as some form of sexual indicator and attractant.

Because the humans' scent perception is on a fairly low level they do not realize that, however much they may try to disguise the visible signs of their mood and reactions, their change in smell, due to perspiration produced over such a wide area of their bodies, is an immediate indicator to any canine. However brave a front they may put upon it, it is as easy as gnawing a bone to know when a human is afraid for the acrid smell can be overpowering. But, since one human's rate of glandular secretion may differ from another's, it is not possible to produce a quantified scale of assessment.

Many humans are able to interpret our more general forms of communication. They recognize our friendly overtures (although not always welcoming them) and they are usually able to recognize our appeasement gestures; but they do sometimes get things wrong and, when we are totally giving way, think that we are being aggressive, and when we wag our tails, as long as we wag them, assume that we must be happy. Fortunately, some humans are very interested in understanding other species—and they have very carefully tried to understand all other forms of communication and then made their findings available to other humans through their marks on paper. They are not entirely accurate and they have often thought up some very strange reasons to explain why we behave as we do, but at least it is a beginning. In practice, the limitation of human knowledge is some help to us in handling them. If they could read us as well as we can them our position might be considerably less strong.

There are still thousands of our brothers and sisters who have painful and unhappy lives because of humans, but conditions are generally getting better—for humans are so guilty about what they have done to the world and to each other that they adopt a much more responsible attitude to the other species they take into their homes. They make the decision to share their lives with us much more carefully and, having made it, are under much greater pressure to keep their part of the bargain. Make no mistake, our relationship with humans is a bargain, although one made thousands of years ago, and, if it is to work, we have to keep our part of the bargain as much as they must keep theirs. In training your owner you have to keep this in mind.

It would be quite possible for most canines who wished it to become 'top dog' as far as a human pack is concerned, but if you look at situations where this has happened you will see that, in the long run, it has not always been to the dog's advantage. Most humans are quite incapable of following where a dog wants to lead and so, as a result, he or she ends up living a soft, but desperately boring life, and probably indulging in all sorts of petty vices that lead to bad health (especially laziness and eating the wrong kinds of foods which make for overweight, heart conditions and rotten teeth).

If you are living in the wild, and set up with a human, like those wolf cousins who, from time to time, have succoured and adopted human pups, it might be possible to lead them as part of your own pack—but this is not the case for most of us today. We live in a world that humans have made and it is organized to suit them, not us. The digital development of their paws makes it possible for them to do many things much more easily, including the operation of the whole technological support systems that they have evolved. In such a world it is likely to be more efficient to allow the pack leader to be a human. Even in an entirely canine world only a small proportion would be pack leaders so that most of us would never become top dog; there is therefore little loss of pride in accepting the position of number two to a well-trained human.

If you are to be led by a human he must be taught to lead in the areas where you need leadership, and to lead in a way that you can understand. It is as much in this as in making sure that we get what we want from him or her that we must persevere patiently in training our owners.

Most of us need a degree of discipline or we over-indulge ourselves. We want to be well fed, but, if humans provide our food and we do not have to go to all the effort of catching it, there is no need to gorge ourselves. If we have a sweet tooth and eat too many candies our teeth will rot. Our instincts tell us to take what we can when we can— you cannot undo thousands of years of habit so easily— then it is useful to have humans that restrain us when there is more than we need available. If we demand too much attention our humans will have no time to do the other things which they must in order to provide for us. If we indulge our sexuality without control we may end up with a pack that has grown over large. Centuries ago, the pack could have broken into two, and one half found a new territory, but where is there territory to be found today where we could sustain ourselves, except in human homes? I am not suggesting a masochistic life of self-denial; but it is easier to be restrained with a human to do the restraining, and it is more fun to connive at an irregular treat than to be pampered all the time. After all, getting round most humans is very easy. A soulful eye filled with a plaintive look and you are more than half-way there. And do you remember that gesture you used to make as a tiny puppy asking for more food when your mother brought a meal home to regurgitate it for you? Perhaps you were human-reared and have no actual remembrance, but it is part of your instinctive inheritance. It began in reaching up to take food from her mouth, first with your mouth and then

53

with your paw, and eventually you used to raise a paw as a gesture of welcome and anticipation. Try going up to a human, sitting down before him and raising a front paw in a gesture just like that. He will almost certainly take it and give it a shake, for it is a greeting gesture for humans, too, although one which has evolved for quite different reasons and in quite a different way. He will think that you are behaving like a human—and nothing seems to please humans more.

Careful, there is a danger here! You are *not* a human. *You* are a dog—and if you are going to be happy you should never forget it. You need to live as a dog. It is all very well adapting slightly to fit within a human pack, but if you deny all your instincts and ancestry you are going to end up a mad dog and, humans will think, a bad dog. In your first days with a new owner try to work out why the human wants a dog. There is always a reason for any animal choosing to live with an animal of a different species. Earlier I have tried to give you some advice about the selection of a human, but all too often we have no choice. We have to live with humans and we have to join a pack that is forced upon us, so there is not much you can do about it. But the humans have consciously decided that they want us with them, although not necessarily for the reason that they believe. They may need a dog to help with some specific task: hunting, guiding, herding. They may want you as a watchdog to deter trespassers. They may have some idea that looking after you will teach their pups a sense of responsibility. They may just think of you as a status symbol, because your breed is currently expensive and fashionable. Or they may simply be in desperate need of companionship, of something to love.

In most cases a human's choice will not be a clear-cut decision in favour of one of these reasons but rather a combination of several of them. Whatever the reason, fortunately most of us find ourselves in homes where we rapidly become a warmly loved part of the family pack. Love is a human expression which is a little hard to understand. Many humans think that we love them in return—and perhaps we do—but I find it impossible to say what it really means. Certainly we follow the leader we have accepted, unless that leader relinquishes his role, and we are loyal to the pack to which we belong. We miss the company of our pack fellows, and of our pack leader especially, as we would miss the company and warmth of canine packmates. We are jealous of our rights and show jealousy when they are infringed. We would risk our own safety if our pack were threatened and were there no way of outfacing the danger. Perhaps it is all these things that the humans mean by 'love', for they are the reactions which they show to the ones they say they love, and they are certainly not such common virtues among men as they are among dogs.

Some of us are better equipped to fit into certain pack situations than into others, an aspect I have already touched upon. Apart from problems such as adult size it is largely a matter of professional skills. The problem is that, if you have not been well briefed when a tiny puppy, you probably know little about the capabilities bred into you—you may not even know your breed, or breed-mix if you are a mongrel. However, you will probably discover that you have an urge to do certain things: to chase fast-moving animals, for instance (that may mean you are a gaze-hound); or follow trails (scent hounds); you may have a passion for digging animals out of holes (terriers); or for rounding up everybody else (herd dogs); or your instincts may make you go into a rigid stance in line with the location of hidden game (pointers); or want to fetch fallen animals for your human (spaniels and retrievers). We all have these compulsions to some degree but in certain dogs they will be particularly strong; they should recognize them in themselves and indicate as much to their owners for dogs must fulfil their instincts if they are to be happy. Since the human may actually know more about your ancestry than you, he or she may already be aware that you will want to pursue these activities. Show him how

55

good you are at them and, with luck, he will join you in a training programme to learn his own role and make you even more skilful so that you gain immense satisfaction instead of being frustrated because your instinctive skills are ignored.

Putting your abilities across to your owner is simply a matter of demonstrating them—but take care not to break any of his or her rules in doing so. A terrier who shows off his digging on the drawing-room carpet or in the middle of the rose-bed may call down retribution instead of lively interest. Judge both place and time with care.

Some dogs will have no need to make such demonstrations. Their humans will have chosen them very carefully because blood and behaviour indicate a high skill potential. Those dogs may not have so comfortable a life, but they will have an active one for they will be kept at work or in training almost every day. They will certainly earn their keep. It is only fair that *all* dogs should try to do so by performing the tasks given them as thoroughly as they are able. That is all part of our bargain with the humans. They feed us, give us shelter and medical care (and the cost of these is very high today). Imagine how much it costs to feed a large dog considering the amount of meat he eats each day—and small ones eat quite a lot too! It works out at quite a big chunk of the human's income. It is only reasonable that we try to contribute something in return.

As well as work tasks you will find that humans encourage you to do a number of tricks. These may be displays of physical skill and daring—such as jumping through hoops, perhaps burning ones—or they may be playing at being human—such as walking on two legs. There is no harm in this but sometimes the human will take this anthropomorphism too far. If your human actually tries to treat you too much like a human you must firmly refuse to respond. Always remember that you are a dog and train your owner to do the same.

Collars are useful for carrying a means of identification (tattoos are even smarter, but not all humans know that a dog without a collar may have his name and number tattooed upon his or her skin), but they are as far as you should go in dressing up except in special circumstances. Practical covers, to keep your coat clean at shows or to keep a short-haired dog warm, are acceptable. A few breeds, such as the Yorkshire terrier, may have to put up with having ribbons tied in their fur for shows, but dressing up in human-type clothes should be ruled out. If you have to put up with nappies and plastic pants (I have never seen them but have heard rumours that they exist) then I suspect that that is your fault for not doing your business in the proper place and the sooner you get your life reorganized the better. If you find your owner treats you too much like a human baby, even if you enjoy it, jump out of his arms and have a good bark to remind him that you are a dog. Playing at being baby can give you an easy life at first, but you will soon discover that humans are not able to cope when you suddenly decide to be a dog again— so make sure that it is clear that being baby is only a game.

Communication with humans requires patience. Since most of them lack the instinctive understanding which we dogs share you must consciously tell them when you want things and remind them when they forget their duties. Fortunately, they are relatively good at following obvious visual signals. The simplest way of showing your needs is to present some visual indication. If you want to go out of a closed room sit by the door and look at it—a gaze directed at the knob which the human must turn is most effective. (If there is a handle instead of a knob you may be able to depress it with a paw, then, if the door opens away from you, you can let yourself through.) If you feel that a meal-time is overdue go to your empty bowl and sniff at it. If you need water, follow the same procedure. If exercise time is being forgotten fetch your lead and take it to your walking partner.

Naturally, such mimetic action is useless if it goes unobserved. You should first attract human attention either by paw touch (on the knee, for instance, if the human is in a sitting position) or vocally. Wild dogs have a range of yowls, yelps and howls with which to convey distant messages of warning, which are part of their hunting intelligence and which may be of a sexual nature but—from where I do not know—we domestic canids have learned to make a sharper, harsher sound: the bark. It is ideal for attracting attention but should not be over-used. Except when giving urgent warning of intruders it should be dropped as soon as attention has been gained and a more gentle pleading tone used to request the performance of the task which you require done. Add a liquid look in the eye and most humans will find you irresistible.

Humans usually understand the more basic of our vocalizations, although they frequently misinterpret a warning growl as anger or as the precursor of attack when we are only politely asking them to keep their distance or to stop doing something painful or annoying to us. They are frequently annoyed by howling and are not properly aware of this as a warning of danger. It is often our reaction to sounds and other stimuli which the human already expects and of which he or she knows the origin but we do not; the human cannot therefore understand why we are crying 'danger'. They do appreciate that our barking when on guard is to scare away intruders, although they do not necessarily understand that we must bark to keep off those who may threaten us, even if they are creatures which the humans would tolerate. They recognize our happy barks at play with them, but do not like us to get over-excited—for then they may begin to feel that they are losing their leadership and may even begin to smell of fear. This is one of the problems if you have a more dominant personality than your human.

Cries of pain, our usual shrill call in reaction to a sudden injury, and the low moan or whine with which we react to more lasting pain (or to the lack of attention when we are very young) are easy for humans to interpret. These sounds and those of pleasure and excitement are probably close enough to those made by human pups before they learn word sounds for the adult human to retain an instinctive understanding of them.

Try to establish a regular timetable for both yourself and your human. You will then have a pattern around which the rest of your lives can be arranged. Once fixed, beware of trying to anticipate these established times. Too many dogs, anxious and impatient, anticipate the time for food or exercise and begin to ask for it at ever earlier times. This can only lead to a situation where the timetable breaks down and you will not be able to rely on anything, or, if the human is experienced in canine ways, may lead to your requests being ignored and even perhaps to some kind of punishment in reprisal.

For adults an ideal daily pattern might begin with a long morning walk, giving an opportunity first thing to relieve yourself after the night indoors. The humans can then set off on their own daily expedition leaving you to have a snooze after the healthy exercise. When they return in the evening they can prepare your meal and you can eat as they settle down to their own dinner or supper. Then you can have another outing (once again being able to attend to nature's needs) before you and they retire to bed. Many humans will make this evening stroll a social outing for themselves, often calling in at a 'pub'. In common with their liking us to display 'human' traits it seems to please them if we share some of their strong-smelling beverage— and some dogs do grow to like it—but beware! Too much of it can dull the senses and weaken muscle control to way below the human level. This drink comes in several flavours but all have the effect of making one feel rather good. It sometimes brings out one's belligerence and, worse, it can make you ill in the stomach. If your human drinks a lot of it try to keep off the stuff yourself, or take only a very little for politeness' sake, for you may find that it is your responsibility to get your human home.

For the most part, humans expect us to follow their lead, and as pack members accepting them as leader we will do so if personal needs are not so pressing as to take

59

precedence. There are, however, occasions when the role becomes, at least in part, reversed. We may, for instance, be left in charge of very young humans when the pack leader is unable to supervise them. It is then our duty to prevent them from being molested and to warn other humans if they stray into danger. This variety of guard duty is no more than part of pack defence but, for the professional dog who specializes in working with the blind, there is a need to actually observe, think and react for the humans. The blind person does not stop being pack leader (although it would be difficult to believe that a blind canine could lead a pack in the wild) for the *final* decisions upon actions will be his, but the dog must be his eyes and lead him everywhere.

Not every dog is suitable for working with the blind. It is a job that requires dedication and concentration. A dog distracted by a bitch in season, a challenge from a neighbour or a tantalizing smell from a cornerpost will be unable to do his work properly. For these reasons females are nearly always chosen for this work since the temptations are somewhat less for them and they are often of a generally gentler disposition. In fact, a majority of guide dogs these days are neutered to avoid the complications that sexuality brings. Both dog and human have to undergo very special training, but through this they probably develop a much closer rapport than exists in any other cross-species relationship. The dog must be not only highly aware of all possible dangers but respond to them with an awareness of the size, manoeuvrability and vulnerability of a blind human. Uneven surfaces, steps, slopes, kerbs, narrow spaces (whether between buildings, vehicles, street furniture or people), doorways, lifts, overhead obstructions, and so on, must all be assessed for the safety of the dog's ward. Decisions must be taken on when it is safe to cross a road or negotiate another dangerous territory, yet it is important not to lead a blind partner too forcefully. The dog has always to try to offer information to the human and let the human decide where he wants to go—it always aids human confidence to give them the impression that they are in charge.

Guiding the blind is one of the most satisfying occupations for any dog of a suitable temperament and a dog of integrity will be proud to be chosen for this work. We are all far happier if we know that we are making a positive contribution to our pack. Although those with specific inherited skills have an advantage we can all find a useful role. To be efficient at this may involve some training on our own part and, unless we go through the vital formative period of our life with older dogs as our mentors, this means training supervised by humans.

Elsewhere in this book I have discussed the young pup's first arrival in his new home. Many juveniles may be exposed to their first training by humans at that point and it would help them considerably if they could be prepared for the ways in which humans try to carry out this operation.

Whatever they are trying to teach us, humans attempt to establish what they want done by a system of punishment and reward. (There are exceptional bullies who treat others, humans and canines alike, with violence, but fortunately I myself have never encountered one as a pack leader. If you do I can only suggest that this is a case when it is worth the risks involved in trying to escape and find a new pack and territory.) Reward is easy enough to recognize, whether it be by way of food, a favourite game, a pleasant grooming activity or other attention. From a pack leader it may be simply a display of approval. Punishment is more difficult to recognize. It is not usually the cold-haunched disdain, nor the vicious scrapping of the pack but more often a hard blow and a verbal scolding. This should not be misconstrued as a fighting challenge on the human's part but something much more like our own low-level aggression signals warning against doing a thing again—for after all, once done, what point is there in revenge? Some humans may be revengeful (they do not have as well-adjusted an appeasement system as we have), just as some dogs, having reached a pitch of anger, cannot restrain themselves; but most quickly recognize our postures and expressions of submission and desist, delivering only a verbal admonition which you can identify by their tone of voice.

What is most difficult to grasp is the way in which humans indulge in their 'punishment' behaviour for no apparent reason. You may perhaps have just come running up to them to answer their call, tail awag and pleased as Punch's dog at having kept a stranger off pack territory, when whack, they let you have it! It was not until I was quite grown up that I realized that many humans have a strange delay in their behaviour pattern: they are actually administering a punishment for something you have *stopped* doing (the stranger was not an intruder, for example, and should have been accepted), not for what you are doing at the moment. Since you are already thinking about your pleasure at running up to your human and expect a welcome and praise for promptly answering his or her call this can be very confusing, especially for young puppies, and may result in some decidedly neurotic adults who cannot cope with always being punished when they do things which they feel sure are going to please. It would help so much if humans could make certain that they match the action to the deed, the rebuke to the misdemeanour. Then, as soon as the puppy changes to doing what they want, they should show their pleasure with appropriate praise. Any bitch knows that this is the simplest way to teach a litter. Why do humans, who profess to have much bigger brains than ours, seem to be so stupid?

There is another way in which humans often confuse their instructions. They will use more than one vocal signal to mean the same thing. When they want you to go to them they may say 'Come here!' or 'Here!' or 'Come!' or even 'Heel!' It they would keep to one expression it would be much easier to follow their meaning. If they establish the word 'Here' we will still understand if they say 'Come here' for they will still be using the signal word, but if they say 'Come' without adding the signal word how do they expect any dog to understand them? Naturally, some of us see through their inefficiency and identify the different signal as having an identical meaning, but this does not help in the even more confusing situation when they incorporate the signal word in an instruction intended to be contrary to its meaning. They may, for instance, say 'Do not come here', which in human voice signals means 'Stay', but since the signal 'Here' (and 'Come' if you have learned both) is included a dutiful dog will automatically do exactly the opposite to what the human wishes. Humans can think very complicated thoughts but, in many ways, their brains seem to find simple logic extremely difficult to handle.

Humans also have a habit of calling to attract your attention and then, when you have located their general direction, suddenly going quiet and standing still so that you have no way of working out where they are unless they are within scenting distance. Perhaps it is because so many humans use artificial ways of seeing. They watch things which are not really happening in glass boxes and they put round transparent discs in front of their eyes attached to wires around their ears which apparently improve their vision. They also have similar devices which they actually place beneath their eyelids, although I do not think all humans wear them. With these aids they can apparently see over longer distances than us and perhaps they forget that without them it is impossible to distinguish stationary objects clearly.

There are courses on which you can take your human to have him or her trained in communication but, unfortunately, as in so many things, these are organized by humans and it is up to your human to recognize the need to go to them. Some dogs have found that by exaggerating the lack of communication and deliberately ignoring even the instructions of their pack leader they have been able to demonstrate to their human that he or she should go on such a course—but sometimes this misfires and the dog could find himself on a specialized canine training course instead. Such a course can be very satisfying in itself, for working with skilled and understanding humans is a pleasure, but this does nothing to improve the performance of your own pack leader and, if anything, only increases your frustration since it will have been demonstrated how efficiently some human beings can work if they take the trouble.

The ideal situation, it seems to me, is that encountered by professional herding dogs. Not only do they have satisfying work, in which they are given a large measure of autonomous responsibility, but they also have a pack to control as clear deputy leader and a really skilled human pack leader who can communicate through an exact and detailed system of body signals and either vocal or whistle calls. When work is over these dogs usually share a happy home life with the human house-pack and evolve a warm and affectionate rapport with them.

7 KEEPING FIT

A lot of nonsense is talked about keeping fit, especially by humans. For themselves they lay down correct weights for heights, and for us they speak in terms of distances over which we should be exercised. Some will decree that every dog should be taken out walking for at least an hour each day, others that all except the very smallest need a walk of three to four miles minimum daily. No puppy under four months should be exercised at all, warn others; or they claim that large dogs should not go for walks until they are over six months old. Why cannot they just use their common sense? Of course, a pup should not be overtaxed. In its enthusiasm to keep up with its human it will easily strain itself. Most of its food intake, in fact, goes in building up its body. Moreover, very young pups get quite enough exercise playing with mother and their siblings. They are trying out all the physical potential of their limbs. Romping around the house and garden will be all the exercise they need for the first few months of their lives. If they live in a flat or gardenless home they are going to be taken out for toilet purposes regularly and those excursions will give them a chance to stretch their legs.

If you belong to one of those breeds which specialize in running and racing you may become very frustrated if you are not given the chance to indulge in violent exercise, but you do not necessarily require all that exercise to keep physically fit, provided that you do not eat too much and become overweight. A very boisterous dog will want to work off some of his surplus energy, and can do that by going out and rushing around somewhere safe from cars and other dangers. If you are a big dog, such as a Great Dane, you will need more space than a small dog, but you will not necessarily need to go for longer walks or to spend more time at exercise. There is no need to copy those humans who spend all their spare time lifting heavy weights to develop bulging muscles or run around in circles trying to prove that they can get nowhere faster than anyone else.

The important thing is to have a regular exercise pattern. The human who will take you for a twelve-mile ramble each day for six weeks and then keep you cooped up in a flat, except for toilet outings, for the next six months, is asking for difficulties. Try to insist upon, say, a daily fifteen-minute trot around the block or to the park and back. If you have your human on a lead and treat the routine walk as a matter of course they are unlikely to persist in trying to cut it short. They may find it a little boring going along the same route every day, not appreciating that you are checking up on all the 'news' of the neighbourhood as you go round, so if they want to vary where they go do not discourage it, provided that they do not chicken out of coming at all.

If there is a place where you can run free for a time, all the better; but do not stretch the time too far, and return when you are called. If you keep your humans waiting they may change their minds about letting you run without the leash, and trying to drag humans along at a fun pace, or into some of the places you will want to investigate, is almost impossible: they are far too slow and bad at manoeuvring through undergrowth and awkward spaces.

Cats seem to be quite happy rushing around on their own but most of us find solitary exercise extremely boring. It can be fun if we can range free with another dog, but with almost everywhere taken over by irresponsible and dangerously reckless humans and machines, that kind of opportunity is rare for town and suburban pets. Most of us naturally prefer a properly organized outing with a human to exercise to give some point to the expedition. Rushing around the backyard on our own, however big the backyard may be, is just not on. You have no need to feel that this is a selfish attitude, for humans usually do need the exercise. Most of them get far too little and easily become overweight from eating too much; those who do not will usually enjoy the exercise anyway.

Many of these humans who volunteer for exercise make a great fetish of 'getting out in the open-air'. This is fine if by that they mean being out in an open strip of countryside, up in the mountains, down by the sea, or even in a large city park with plenty of trees and grass to combat the polluted atmosphere—but a walk on city streets, particularly when there is a lot of traffic about, may be good for exercise but hardly provides fresh air. It may be better in the early hours of the morning when the traffic is at its least, but, even if human noses with their low sensitivity and extra height above the pavement do not notice it, we have to put up with the worst of the dust and dirt that blows about and the fumes that come from car exhausts at just our level. Night walkers may have to be prepared to defend their human against muggers and other miscreants and are not so likely to join in a human-canine social life, so I personally prefer to keep such late excursions mainly for toilet exercises. But I am lucky and live close enough to a big park to get some energetic morning exercise after only a brief scramble through the traffic.

Some dogs are spoiled and avoid the worst of the pavement pollution because they ride by car to a park or country area, but if that is not possible, there is less harm in getting your exercise in off-street areas, even indoors if there is space, away from the busy traffic routes.

When you are out in the open, if your human does not like running and chasing games then let him take a rest. It is not your fault if, having got him out to take exercise he needs, he does not take advantage of it. Instead, try taking a small branch or other object to him in your mouth. Most humans catch on pretty quickly and will throw it for you, and then you have something to rush after and find. Humans like to think that they are in control of this game; however many times you stop playing with them and leave the branch, trotting up to tell them that it is time to change to something else or to go home, they still seem to think that it is they who have brought the game to an end. Perhaps it is just as well not to disillusion them. Humans seem to enjoy this throwing game and will often learn to bring a ball or other easy projectile with them with which you can keep them happy throwing time and again (it is less effort for them than hurling a stick) while you get in plenty of rushing around.

You should make sure that you get all kinds of exercise so that as many muscles as possible are kept in trim. Running, leaping, turning, swimming (if you can get the chance) and rolling will help to bring them all into play so that a sudden move does not find a particular muscle under-used and strained by the new demand. Do not overdo things. Too much exertion will put a strain upon the heart so show your humans that you mean it when a rest is needed. Unless you have already delayed them and made them late for some other engagement they will probably be delighted at being given an excuse to rest themselves: most humans are pretty lazy creatures.

Whilst out-of-doors there are many irritations and dangers other than that of the motor car. Even as you run through apparently harmless grass or along country paths you may get a thorn in your paw or a seed may lodge itself in your ear. Your fur can pick up burrs and other prickly things that work into the coat and scratch the skin as well as tangle up the hairs. Indoors, as well as out, there are sharp things like tin cans and broken glass which can inflict wounds. On our own we have to rely upon scratching with our toe-nails, biting to remove foreign bodies and licking to clean our wounds, but as part of the human pack we have the help of their agile fingers to remove any harmful particles and their medicines to treat our wounds. Fortunately, most owners notice if you get into that kind of trouble but, nevertheless, it is advisable to bring any injuries or difficulties to their attention by showing them the place which is troubling you. Try to be patient if they are helping you, even if they have to hurt you more to treat the injury. If you have been seriously hurt it will be a shock to you and you probably will not be able to control your reactions and may even bite the hand that helps you. You must not therefore be surprised if the humans go so far as to bind your jaws with a bandage or with one of the pieces of cloth they wear around their necks and their waists. It is just to stop you unintentionally hurting them.

Some humans have been specially trained in caring for the injured and the sick. They may come to you or you may be taken to see them by your humans. These veterinarians, or vets, as humans call them, usually have a room where you have to wait with other dogs, felines and many different species, including animals who have brought their humans for treatment (they usually seem to be suffering from nervous disorders). They are all sick in some way so you must suppress any reaction towards prey species or other natural antagonists—humans would think it most unsporting of you to take advantage of another animal's sickness. It always seems to amaze humans how successfully most of us can suppress any antagonisms in such circumstances, but when you are vulnerable yourself it is no time to pick a fight.

Vets know a lot about all kinds of conditions: injuries, infections which make you feel ill, parasites, internal upsets caused by eating or drinking things which do not agree with you or even poison your whole system, and all those little aches and pains that we suffer from as we get older. You should try to put your trust in them and help them as much as possible.

When we are sick we instinctively withdraw from company to rest and allow our bodies to combat what is wrong, but with this trained medical help you should be prepared to do exactly the opposite, to allow yourself to be handled and inspected in the most intimate way. The vets will often push a thin glass tube right up your rectum— apparently it tells them how hot you are inside.

Sometimes, because your pack leader or the other humans in your pack lack specialist knowledge and experience they may do something to you when you are injured or ill which gives you more pain. You should gently let them know with a soft moan, or a growl if they continue, and insist that they desist. With the veterinarians your reactions will give him additional information and if he accidentally hurts it will be in the cause of finding something out or putting something right. You should still react but understand that he may still have to go on hurting you a little. In fact, vets and their assistants are skilled in ways of holding you so that you cannot struggle and have to put up with what they do, and they can even make you become unconscious by giving you a drug if you struggle too strongly or your pain makes it difficult for you to cooperate.

Sometimes a dog 'comes to' to discover that his skin appears to have been cut and then sewn together again— apparently the vets can open you up and put things right inside. If you think this has happened try to take things gently for a few days or you may undo their work. In such cases your humans will probably do their best to make sure that you keep fairly still and do not run around or jump too quickly until the healing is well advanced.

Except for bandages and dressings for wounds and splints and plasters for broken bones the vets' treatment usually consists of creams and drops to apply externally, medicines or pills which you have to swallow, or sometimes a needle which they push into you and from which they squeeze some liquid beneath your skin. This pricks a little but does not usually hurt very much. Sometimes it is this needle that makes you lose consciousness but veterinarians have to be very careful what they do and have a strict code of honour so you should be prepared to trust them. Not many other humans are skilled at giving these 'injections', but your own human will be responsible for giving you pills and medicines when you get home. Some dogs really dislike taking pills but I feel it is pointless to resist, not only because they are intended to do you good but because a pill that you hold in your mouth, refusing to swallow, in the hope that you will find a chance to spit it out, will often produce a most unpleasant froth, worse than taking the pill itself. Sometimes humans will mix pills or medicines in powder form with your food in the hope that in your hurry to eat you will not notice the medication. Pretend that you do not—humans like to feel that they have succeeded in outwitting you—and, since they will often give you a particularly favourite food to mask their trick, you end up with a better dinner, too.

8 KEEPING TRIM

Most of us are not very worried by what we look like, although it can be of prime importance to our humans. But, nevertheless, we do not like being uncomfortable, and keeping our coats clear of bits of plants, lumps of mud and sticky messes and ensuring that our unhairy areas are clean all helps to make life more pleasant. Our ancestors used to do all this themselves, relying upon scratching with their nails, rubbing up against tree trunks and other firm objects, rolling on the ground, biting, shaking, licking and taking the occasional dip in a clear stream to keep themselves in trim. Of course, we can still do these things—and licking is probably still the best way of making sure that our private parts are clean—but our lives are made much easier because our humans are prepared to spend quite a lot of time in grooming us. And so they should, for it is because of their interference that many of us have fur lengths and physical features not found in the original wild canids which increase the problems of keeping our bodies comfortable and clean.

The dog living in the wild moults according to the seasons, his hair growing longer and thicker for the colder months and being shed as the days grow warmer. We domestic dogs usually live in artificially heated homes where the lengthening of the day by artificial lighting interferes with our bodies' natural response to the clear-cut pattern of the seasons. Since humans generally object to finding our hairs all over their carpets and furniture they have to be prepared to get to work with brush and comb to keep our coats free of falling hair. Grooming is an enjoyable activity, like vigorous stroking most of the time, and something to be welcomed. Only dogs who are accidentally injured when very young or otherwise frightened during grooming have any problems getting used to it and, with a little patience on the part of your human, even these neuroses should be soon overcome. It is strange that, although they must realize that we enjoy being brushed, so many humans do not appreciate that it is stroking, not hitting, we enjoy. For centuries humans seem to have been convinced that all dogs are born masochists and that their 'patting' gives us pleasure.

Not all dogs require the same attention, we should each be groomed according to our breed and physical characteristics and our humans should equip themselves with the appropriate brushes and other tools to do it properly (there is a wide range of brushes available to suit our different coats and the methods of our humans). Our fur consists of two coats, an under- and an over-coat (this is more noticeable in long-haired dogs); the longer the over-coat the more detailed the grooming has to be. If your human wants to avoid any hairs on the furniture he must find the time to groom you every day, but this is not usually necessary unless you are moulting.

A short-haired dog will normally need a brushing only once or twice a week and for this a 'hound glove' (a mitten which fits over the groom's paw) is probably the easiest for most humans to use. It has short stiff bristles on the palm which will give a lively massage to skin and muscles without scratching the skin, as well as removing loose dead fur. After grooming with it a final rub down with an old nylon stocking will give the coat an extra gloss.

Long-haired dogs will need more detailed attention. Burrs and other particles as well as tangles will need careful combing from your coat along with the dead hair. With all breeds dead hair can be loosened by massaging, a very pleasant sensation when the human knows how to use his fingers properly. A firm stroking from head to tail with his paw will then work out most of the loose hair.

Unless you are a very big dog, in which case your valet will probably prefer to work on the floor with sheets of newspaper spread around to catch the fallen hair and bits of debris, you will probably find that your human puts you on a table-top for grooming.

Grooming sessions should not stop at just dealing with your coat. Toes and pads should be cleaned between, and excessive hair trimmed away to prevent it knotting or gathering dirt. Nails should be checked to make sure that they are not split or growing too long. If you get plenty of exercise on hard surfaces they will probably be kept well worn down but if not they should be trimmed. Do not be frightened of this. As long as your human uses proper nail clippers and makes sure that he or she keeps well clear of the quick—the upper portion which contains the blood vessels and nerves—you will not feel it at all. Humans cut their own nails, you know, so it's not new to them (though they had best not try to use their own nail scissors on us; we need those specially designed for dogs). In dogs with light-coloured claws it is easy for your human to see where the pink part starts, but if you have dark claws and it does not show you must hope that your humans have some sense, or that their veterinarian has shown them how and where to cut before they try to do it on their own. A properly trimmed nail should just touch the ground when the pads of the toes are flat. Incidentally, life is usually more comfortable if a veterinarian removes the dew claws on the inner-side of the forefeet (and sometimes on the hindfeet as well) when you are only a few days old, although in some breeds they have to be retained if you are to be shown.

Eyes and ears should be inspected and cleaned with a little cotton wool, which may be moistened with olive oil. If you find that brushes scratch the bony parts of your face encourage your groom to wipe them with a cloth. The mouth should be inspected to make sure that it is generally healthy and the teeth checked occasionally for any sign of

74

decay and to ensure that they are not becoming covered by a build-up of tartar. A tartar coating will not generally become a problem until you are past two years old but in some dogs it may then become so heavy that it needs removing every three or four months. Gnawing upon knuckle bones and eating hard biscuits will help to keep your teeth clean.

At your other end soiled mats of hair should be removed and a watch kept on the state of your anal glands. Humans do not have these and I think we might be better without them. Certainly no one seems to know what we were supposed to use them for. They contain a rather ill-scented fluid and maybe we used them in the same way as the skunk: to keep off those who might want to molest us. With the rough diet we would have eaten in the wild the pressure of our faeces passing by them probably helped to empty them and their lubrication perhaps made defecation easier, but contemporary domestic-pack diets have interfered with this process and these glands can fill up and become infected. If you find they are becoming painful and your humans do not notice, you may gain a little relief from rubbing them along the ground or by licking them, but this is of no permanent help. But it may attract the attention of your humans to your condition. Your veterinarian, or your pack-leader if he or she is sufficiently skilled, can express the liquid by pressing carefully upon the glands. Try to put up with the momentary discomfort without complaint—it is well worth it afterwards.

Fleas are another problem that should come to light at grooming sessions, their excreta on your coat forming dirty patches that are easier to see than the fleas themselves. Some dogs claim never to be troubled by fleas, although I am personally inclined to think that they must have very insensitive skins. There is no shame in admitting to having them for they can leap upon you from anywhere—a country lane, a hired limousine, a passer-by or even a visiting archbishop—and provided that you do not let them settle in they need not cause much trouble.

However, if they become established in your home they can require a lot of effort on your human's part to get rid of them.

Presumably our wild brethren just got used to fleas, but most modern dogs find them somewhat of a nuisance. By all means try to catch them yourself (some wits say that they were invented to make sure we get exercise for all our muscles), and do not be discreet; be noticed doing it, so that your humans will become aware of your problem. If they do not notice them at grooming, or see you hunting for them in your fur, or if they do not realize the reason for your frantic scratching, you will just have to hope that a few of the fleas will jump on to them. Dog fleas do not like living upon humans—it is a different species of flea that prefers them—but if one does alight upon a human it will take a bite or two before it finds out that it has made a mistake and starts to look for a source of rich canine blood, quite enough to irritate your human into looking for the culprit.

There are several different kinds of treatment for getting rid of fleas: you may find yourself being dusted with powder, sprayed from an aerosol can or even being given a fleacide dip. Powder is the most usual method used. This treatment can be a little unsettling if you do not know what to expect. Your human (assuming that he or she knows what to do) will spread out some newspaper on the floor, place you in the middle and give you a dusting all over, but particularly on the head, neck and ears and under the legs where the fleas like to congregate. The powder will be rubbed into your coat from your tail forward and then a careful combing with a fine-tooth-comb will clear them out, most of them already dead or dying. Naturally, your human should burn the newspaper and its contents afterwards to kill any fleas that have survived the powder. Your bedding should be either burned or boiled and your basket and any chairs or other places where you lie should be dusted or spread with fleacide and carefully vacuumed. The fleas' eggs, which hatch into little worms and then change into pupae before they reach the adult flea stage, can lodge in crevices and survive for months. The treatment will not affect eggs or pupae so must be repeated at ten-day intervals for several weeks to catch any that are left as they hatch out. If a room which may harbour fleas can be closed up for an hour or so (without you or any other members of the household in it) and sprayed with a thin mist of fleacide, especially along the edges of carpets and in corners and along the bottom of walls, this will prove an even more satisfactory treatment.

Some breeds will need more complicated grooming than a simple brushing. Terriers, such as the Airedale and its wire-haired smaller cousins, should be plucked to keep the coat in trim. The dead coat is removed by the groom carefully plucking it out, gripping the hairs between finger and thumb, or, less effective but sometimes easier, a special stripping knife may be used. Today, terriers are frequently clipped, but this does not help the coat to retain perfect colour or texture.

Poodles are a breed which is regularly trimmed. They do not shed their coats (so do not mess up the furniture), which, if they are not to get over-long, must be cut. It takes some time to get used to the electric clippers that are often used today but in the hands of a skilled groom they are quite safe and there is no need to be frightened. Provided that he has learned to do it properly there is no reason why your human should not do this job at home, but you may be taken to a special 'beauty parlour' to have it done professionally. These experts will comb the hair out first, to make it stand up, then run a clipper over it to reduce its length in a uniform way, change the clipper head to something finer to shave those areas which your human considers the current fashion (there are strict styles laid down for dogs who enter show competitions), and to an even finer head for closer shaving. Poodles will usually then be given a bath and finished off with a final combing after they have been dried.

If your human is excessively conscious of your appearance you may even find that you have to put up with your hair being set in curlers and other fancy 'beauty care'. Yorkshire terriers and other little dogs seem to be the worst sufferers, but, although I would find such fussing intolerable, I believe some of them actually like it.

Baths are something which we all have to put up with occasionally. Mud can usually be brushed off, if your human lets it dry first, and there are dry shampoo powders which can be used for young pups and elderly dogs who should not be bathed, but sometimes the coat gets soiled with things that a thorough washing will remove most easily. Since all of us like a swim it is surprising that many dogs make such a fuss about a bath—perhaps they pick it up from human pups, who sometimes display great distaste for washing of any kind. One of the problems is that humans will insist upon washing our heads first, and that only makes us shake ourselves, an instinctive reaction to dry ourselves over which we have little control. If they would start at the feet and then work along the body from the rear end up, finishing off at our heads, they would find their task much easier and we dogs much more cooperative.

There are special soaps and shampoos made for us but I find the ones made for humans quite satisfactory, as long as detergents and everything containing carbolic are avoided. It is more comfortable, I find, if I am not submerged in the bathwater but stand in the tub with the water level coming below my stomach—you might bark to tell the pourer when to stop. Even better is for your groom to pour lukewarm water over you (still making sure that the water in the tub does not reach a higher level) as he or she soaps you up and then rinses it off. When all the soap has been thoroughly rinsed out a jolly good shake can get the drying started and thoroughly soak the humans in revenge for having been made to stand so still. If the whole family has joined in the ceremony the kids will probably love it—especially if it is the pack leader who gets wettest. Your humans will then rub you down with a rough towel and perhaps finish you off with a hair-dryer. These electric things blow hot air and are really quite pleasant if you forget the noise they make. My owner got me used to off-putting sounds like that when I was very young and I grew up with no fear of them. You are particularly likely to find them used at a beauty parlour. By the way, forget the shaking bit in that kind of establishment— it does not go down well. In any case, you will probably find that the groom has got a towel over you almost before you have had a chance to start!

If you have been swimming in the sea it is a good idea to find some fresh water to wash off the salt for it can set up a skin irritation in some of us. If there is no fresh-water stream flowing onto the beach you may find some humans taking shower-baths that you can share. However, if they are not your own pack be careful whom you choose; most will love the idea, but not all of them, and if you start shaking dry too close to them whilst they are busy towelling themselves they will not be pleased at being soaked again.

9 WINNING PRIZES

Shows are strange occasions. They are one of the few times when we can gather in large numbers yet most of them are by no means the friendly get-togethers that you might expect. They are highly competitive affairs which humans get very worked-up about and which require a lot of preparation beforehand, both in training and in what is to my mind excessive grooming.

We tend to judge other dogs according to their strength and healthiness, their leadership, their skill in hunting, their sexuality and their fun as playfellows, but humans have a whole series of quite different values. At most of these shows their main criteria are concerned solely with our physical appearance. Long ago, humans first valued us for our usefulness to them and judged us according to our skills in the tasks that they found for us. This is not to say that they had no appreciation of what they call beauty in our species, and bore this in mind when arranging our matings. They have always seemed to get a feeling of pleasure and elation from certain arrangements of physical shapes and shades whether in nature or things made by their hands, but, whilst they set us to fight with rats, bears, bulls or against our fellows to compare our valour, or sent us coursing after hares to find the swiftest among us, they did not use our physical appearance as a basis for organized competition until just over a century ago.

In 1835 the British Parliament passed a law which prohibited public bull baiting and dog fights and left a gap in man's sporting scene which was often filled by holding 'leads'—competitive dog matches which led to the development of agreed standards by which the entries could be judged. The coming of railway transport made it possible for dogs and their humans to travel and be entered for competitions in distant places—not always very honestly for they might be entered under more than one description and more than one owner! The first big show was held in Newcastle in 1859 with two categories of entry: pointers and setters, and there was an early emphasis on sporting dogs. The idea of 'shows' in which everything from livestock to farm produce and handicrafts might be judged began to attract more and more of the humans and it became clear that careful organization and established standards were required. In our world this led to the setting up of the Kennel Club in 1873. Since then this organization (of human members: dogs are not allowed to join despite the name) has been responsible for establishing the description of breeds down to fine details and controlled the method of judging in all dog shows. Equivalent organizations have been set up right around the world to control what humans call 'The Fancy'.

Remember that show events are set up by and for our humans, not for us, and do not expect too much from them. Nevertheless, they can prove enjoyable and make a welcome break from routine—sufficiently even to outbalance the longueurs of boredom which form an inevitable part of them and the fuss and fluster that they put our humans into.

There are all kinds of shows from the very smart, such as Crufts great annual show in London, to neighbourhood competitions at church fêtes. The more modest ones sometimes ignore all the rules, allow any dog and owner to compete and offer prizes for things of which the Kennel Club would never approve. Since competitors are likely to be neighbourhood dogs with whom you will have at least a sniffing acquaintance they can become a friendly gettogether with plenty of opportunity for exchange of information. Even the smaller shows organized according

81

to the rule book, especially when held out-of-doors or under canvas, often give one a chance to appraise the available canine talent and, if your natural fancy tends to your own breed, a gesture in the direction of a likely mate may get your humans talking and lead to action later.

Although dog shows (despite the name) are really human shows, run according to their rules for their enjoyment, there is no reason for you not to enter into the spirit of them—although not to such an extent that you become as snooty and stand-offish as some owners. If you are to make the most of shows you must understand what they demand of both dog and owner and be prepared to put in quite a lot of effort beforehand.

The most usual kind of show is organized by breed, and a set of human judges select a dog which they consider the best example of each breed according to the description or 'standard' which they have decided is ideal. That interpretation of the ideal may change considerably over the years as the humans change their taste in long noses or short noses, big feet or small ones, and it may even vary considerably from judge to judge. The ideal is usually based almost entirely upon physical appearance, often an appearance resulting from a deliberate distortion introduced by breeding for an exaggerated look. I am glad to say that in recent years veterinary practitioners and many more enlightened humans have turned against the kind of breeding which has led to physical abnormalities and health problems for many unfortunates in such squat-faced breeds as the pugs and Pekinese.

Naturally, entrants have to be in the peak of condition as well as matching closely to the ideal, or they will have no chance of winning. Usually there will be a further competition at the show between all the breed winners to select a champion which is considered the finest example of canine breeding in the show. There may be other classes of competition too, as at many lesser shows where dogs of no specific breed may compete and everyone can have a chance of appealing to the judge's taste.

In addition to the beauty shows there are other kinds of competition in which we are allowed to show off our special skills in whatever particular area we have chosen—skills which are often closely related to our ancestry. These include gun-work, racing, defence and detection, or competitions in liaison between human and dog to find the pair which show the closest understanding and cooperation. Humans call this last group 'obedience trials'. However, that is something of a misnomer for, although it is really they who are being tested and they who usually gain the prizes, it is we dogs who are expected to carry out the instructions.

The professional dog requires long and close working with his human to shine in sheep-dog work and other such special skills and I do not propose to offer any detailed advice in that area beyond a general exhortation to extreme patience with your human partner on whom, since he or she must work within the very strict rules of the competition, the onus for developing the training programme must depend. I can, however, offer the knowledge that comes from long experience to those who wish to shine in pedigree shows, in popular competitions and in obedience trials.

First, let us face up to the fact that some dogs are just not cut out for competitions. In beauty shows they may have no hope of success because of some 'fault' in their appearance. They may be too high-spirited or impatient ever to settle down to the rigours of a show day. On the other hand, there are some dogs who spend their whole lives going to shows. These are the dogs owned by professional breeders who need to prove the quality of their strain. Many of them are kept as kennel dogs, a rather restricted existence compared with that of the family dog but one which has its compensations in the closeness of canine company and avoidance of the worst extremes of petting.

In addition to an excellent conformation to breed standard a show candidate must have a confident disposition for he or she must be poised, alert and unruffled in the show ring, yet be content to put up with many hours of boredom on the show benches and travelling to and from the showground. These dogs must endure long grooming sessions in preparation for and at the show and remain unaffected by the nervous excitement of their humans. They must calmly tolerate considerable handling by the show judges who will want to feel their bone structure and inspect them thoroughly, including mouth and teeth. No one should imagine that they can go to a show without any preparation and not show the strain in their behaviour.

A primary requirement is to get used to travelling—but this is an essential for most dogs whether they go to shows or not. Then you must get used to being handled by and paraded before strangers (without relaxing your defensive mechanisms concerning territory, property and the safety of your humans). Thirdly, you must accustom yourself to the strain of lying in a restricted area without being distracted by the other dogs around, and by the humans peering at you, eager to see such a fine specimen (although some members of the public may make remarks that reveal their ignorance of your qualities), and without showing the boredom which can so easily overcome you in such circumstances. Meditate upon some restful image to keep your mind calm and occupied: an evening lying before the fire rather than a country walk, which might accidentally lead to over-excitement. Try not to drop off to sleep, for then you might suddenly be awakened and in those first few seconds of waking instinctively do something which would count against you. Always be ready and aware of the approach of the white-coated judges who have to be shown all your best qualities. Professional breeders create plenty of opportunities for their charges to practise show conditions, and you should try to do the same, even if your human does not really appreciate the problems involved.

At a show you will also have to display your qualities by parading in a judging ring, your human, or his representative, walking with you at the other end of the leash. Judges like to view you proceeding at a smart trot with the lead hanging slack between you and your human. You must neither pull nor hang back. This needs plenty of practice to ensure that you and your human keep together and look to your best advantage. In this display of elegance and deportment different breeds look best in different gaits and it is up to your human to discover what is required of you by ·watching other shows and then teaching the appropriate gait to you.

To look your best you will be very carefully groomed and may have to suffer the indignity of travelling coats and covers, or even your fur in curlers, until just before the show, and then have to submit to a final beauty treatment. In addition to shampoos, brushing and combing there are all kinds of ruses which some humans use to remove or conceal stains and improve coat condition, especially on light-furred dogs. If you have already had plenty of trial runs you should be able to take all this in your stride. What you must *not* do, or all that effort and patience will be wasted, is to get dirty again (hence the wraps and covers). If the weather is not good and the show set up out-of-doors be extra careful to avoid getting muddy, and even indoors do not roll around on the floor. To prevent this you may find that your human carries you everywhere until show-time or makes you stay only in the area covered by a clean sheet on the ground.

If you are competing in intelligence and training trials instead of simple beauty competitions do not expect to get off very much more lightly. Although your appearance will not be the main criterion your human will want you to look your finest (or at least what he or she thinks is your finest) and you may well have to submit to almost as much grooming and fuss. With the best humans even that can become an enjoyable experience.

In this kind of competition, however well rehearsed you feel you are, always give the impression that you are listening carefully—and it is wise actually to do so for there might be a sudden change in the programme required of you, or the sequence may not be the one you have been led to expect. Be careful not to anticipate any of the instructions given—you are supposed to follow your human, not show how much better you know the routine. Discipline and control are far more important than speed of understanding.

You will find that the preparation for this kind of competition is usually great fun and will certainly give you more than your normal share of your human's attention. If he is sensible he will let you master one thing at a time and go on to something else only when you have got that one thing right. But don't be offended if your individual lessons are short; in practice it is easier to learn from frequent short lessons than from long ones with a gap of several days between. Make the most of all this specialist training and, when it comes to the actual competition, remember that it is your human that has to get the credit, so do everything to show him off to the best advantage.

Some of the obedience trials are for working dogs only or for members of household packs who have developed a strong amateur talent in a professional discipline. Police dog trials and those for working sheep-dogs are very restricted categories which should be entered only by the very proficient, but the tracking and retrieving work which is required in some of the other tests should be within the capabilities of us all.

The great advantage of such competitions over that of beauty shows is that any dog can participate: lineage and looks are irrelevant provided that you can carry out the necessary manoeuvres to the instructions of your human or a professional handler.

AN APPENDIX
FOR HUMANS

The foregoing text is intended for the canine reader but has much in it to guide the human owner in the relationship with his or her dog. However, given the nature of the authorship there are inevitably some points not covered which it would be useful for the owner to know. The publisher has therefore added the following information which, while not exhaustive, will supplement some of the gaps in the canine text.

Keeping Your Dog Fit

Your dog's health is your responsibility. Changes in behaviour or any feeling that the animal is off-colour should lead to closer investigation to see if there is something wrong. Grooming sessions should include a general physical check-up for disorders and injuries.

Constipation and diarrhoea may be due to a change of diet or a momentary gastric upset. If you see a dog straining it may well be trying to urinate rather than defecate, and its failure to pass motions will not necessarily be noticed unless you always supervise its toilet expeditions. A little olive oil is the safest laxative, and starving for a day the best way of treating diarrhoea. If either diarrhoea or constipation persists it may be a symptom of some more serious condition.

Dogs eat a lot of meat so that their breath will not always be as sweet as you might wish, but if it is really bad this may be a sign of tooth trouble, a gastric disorder or kidney problems.

Try always to report accurately on changes in a dog's condition and when they happened. Keep a record card with dates of inoculations, treatments and their details and illnesses—and, of course, your vet's telephone number and address.

Carefully follow your veterinarian's instructions on nursing and treatment. Make sure that you know exactly what is needed—your vet would much rather take the time to explain again than have the wrong treatment carried out.

Good nursing does not mean making a fuss of the dog; it must be left to rest for long periods and disturbed as little as possible, while still being shown sufficient attention to reassure it of its place in the household. Make sure that it is warm and out of draughts. If it will not relieve itself indoors on a pile of newspapers wrap it up to keep it warm when it goes outside (the coat should protect its chest and abdomen as well as its back and sides). Gentle pressure on the bladder (get your vet to show you how) may encourage it to urinate indoors. Change wet or soiled bedding. Keep the dog clean and well groomed, wiping away eye and nasal discharges and sponging away messes at the rear (drying well afterwards). If you use hot-water bottles to keep the dog warm change them before they get cold and wrap them well to prevent burning. The aim should be to keep temperature constant. Never force food down unless under direct instruction from your vet. In some cases starvation may help and a couple of days without food will do no harm. Follow your vet's instructions if food continues to be rejected and stick to any special diets. Keep water available always, changing it several times a day. If your dog does not drink, spoon a little into the mouth to prevent dehydration. If the dog does not move on its bed it should be turned over every few hours or there may be a risk of pneumonia developing.

Giving Pills and Medicines

Pills and powders can be mixed with your dog's food but if a dog is off-colour there is no guarantee that they will be eaten, or swallowed in the right quantities. It is better to give a pill or powder directly. Sit or stand the dog on a table (it is easier to work standing up), preferably with an assistant to restrain the animal by grasping the forelegs from behind, his arms also controlling the dog's body. Grasp the dog's upper jaw from above, pressing gently with thumb and fingers on either side just behind the upper canine teeth. This should encourage the dog to open its mouth but, if it does not, with the pill already between two fingers of your other hand, push the lower jaw down and place the pill as far back on the tongue as you can reach; rapidly remove the hand and hold the muzzle shut while stroking the dog's throat to encourage it to swallow. Wait for the swallow and check that the pill has gone. Powders can be sprinkled on to the back of the tongue. If you are worried about putting your fingers between the jaws, a patent rod is now available for dropping pills right inside the mouth.

To administer medicines restrain the animal in the same way as described for giving a pill. Have the medicine ready, correctly measured into a spoon, bottle or syringe. Raise the dog's muzzle slightly, holding the mouth closed. Pull out one side of the lower lip to form a pocket into which the liquid can be poured or squirted, a little at a time, and allow it to trickle back into the mouth. Allow the dog to swallow before administering more. Too big a dose in one go may make the dog choke.

Injections

Injections may be subcutaneous (just under the skin) or given directly into muscle tissue. They will usually be administered by a vet or a nursing auxiliary. If it is necessary for you to give injections at home your vet will show you exactly how to do it.

89

Ointments

Ointments are easily licked off. If applied immediately before going out for a walk there is some chance that the dog will be sufficiently distracted to ignore them. If a dog persists in licking off ointment or tearing at a bandage you can prevent it from doing so by making a funnel-shaped collar to fit around its neck. Naturally, this will have to be removed at meal-times.

Bandages and Dressings

Bandaging dogs is not easy and is best done by a vet who can show you exactly how to replace dressings if they need to be changed at home. In an emergency remember that bandaging must be firm but not so tight that it cuts off the circulation. It should spread well beyond the wound and be laid flat. Cover the whole bandage and anchor the edges with adhesive tape to prevent the dog from tearing it off. Bootees taped over the paws will also restrict such activity and an 'Elizabethan' collar around the neck will prevent the dog from biting at the bandages or, in reverse, from scratching a wound or dressing on its head.

Accidents

If your are not sure what to do in the case of an accident restrict yourself to keeping the dog still and warm. If you have to move an injured animal improvize a stretcher (for a small dog a coat or piece of sacking lifted by the corners will serve). If the dog is aggressive tape its muzzle or tie a bandage, necktie or soft belt around it. Get the dog to the vet, or the vet to it, as soon as possible. Local police will help you find the nearest surgery open. In the case of a road accident make sure that approaching traffic is warned so that you are not at risk yourself while attending to the dog, but do not move the animal unnecessarily.

If there is excessive bleeding try to staunch it with a pad

or, if you know how to do it, apply a tourniquet to cut off the blood supply; never leave a tourniquet in place for longer than about twenty minutes. Aspirin can be used as a pain killer with dogs *(but never with cats)*. Only ¼ to ½ tablet should be given to toy dogs, ½ to 1 to miniatures, 1 for medium-sized dogs, such as spaniels, and 2 tablets for the really big breeds. Pain, terror and loss of blood can result in the condition known as shock. Do not give liquids (particularly alcohol) but keep the dog still and warm.

Electric Shock

This will often cause a dog to urinate. Be careful not to step in the puddle or to touch the animal until you have switched off the power supply. If this is impossible, pull or push the dog away from the contact with something that is non-conductive (e.g., a wooden broomstick) and make sure that you are standing on a pad of insulating material. Apply artificial respiration and call the vet.

Artificial Respiration

You may apply artificial respiration to adult dogs by pressing rhythmically upon the rib-cage. With small puppies mouth-to-mouth resuscitation is preferred, since pressure on the ribs may cause permanent damage. If a dog injured in an accident is breathing laboriously it may indicate a ruptured diaphragm, in which case no pressure should be applied in that area until the animal has been examined by a vet.

Drowning

This is uncommon but a dog may become exhausted trying to get out of water where the bank is too sheer. Lift the dog by its hindlegs and allow water to drain out, making sure that its tongue is out of its mouth and there are no obstructions in the mouth or throat. Then begin artificial respiration.

Fractured Limbs

These can be very painful, but do not panic in getting a dog to the vet. Immobilize the animal and try to make it rest so that it cannot make the damage worse. A delay of an hour or two in setting the bone will not be the difference between life and death, although the sooner the dog is given a pain killer the better. Many vets prefer to allow the swelling to subside before they attempt to set the bone.

Stings

Treat both wasp and bee stings with a solution of bicarbonate of soda. If the sting is left in the wound it belonged to a bee. Do not jerk it out with your fingers or you may squeeze more poison into the dog. To pull out the sting, grip it at the base with a pair of tweezers, or a couple of matchsticks. You will certainly need help to hold the dog. If the swelling around the sting becomes very large, and particularly if it is in the mouth and the dog has difficulty in breathing, get the animal to the vet.

Snake Bites

Some snake venom brings death almost instantaneously. If it does not, you have a chance of saving the dog's life for the other poisons travel slowly and you have time to find treatment. Gash the wound open with a sterilized knife (sterilize it by holding it in a clean flame) and allow it to bleed freely to remove some of the poison.

Other Poisons

Take care not to leave toxic substances about; however, sometimes poisonous products have to be used about the house or for rodent control and a dog may accidentally ingest some. If you see it actually eat or drink a poison force it to drink strong salt water or mustard to make it vomit up the poison. If it is already vomiting do not interfere. Ring the vet and tell him the name of the poison and he will suggest an antidote, if you did not find out for yourself when buying such a dangerous product. If you suspect poisoning but do not know the cause you had better get the animal to the surgery.

Burns and Scalds

The most common causes of burns and scalds are walking on hot ashes and spilled hot water. Burns are usually classified as of first, second or third degree. The first are superficial, affecting only the outer layer of skin, causing redness and temporary pain. A dog's fur usually protects him from these except on the face and paw pads. Second degree burns destroy the outer layers of skin and cause blistering. Third degree destroy all the skin layers and may damage the tissue beneath as well.

First degree burns can be treated with a domestic burn lotion, a sunburn cream, for instance, or bathed in cold strong tea. If the skin is entire or blistered but unbroken use very little lotion, leaving the surface dry, and cover with dry gauze and bandage. If the skin is broken use a soothing ointment before bandaging. If the back is scalded apply a large piece of cloth as a bandage, tearing the edges to tie in strips below the body. Scalds may not blister for several days so do not ignore them even if they show no noticeable signs. Serious burns will require rapid veterinary attention. Give the dog aspirin to ease the pain while you contact the vet. Cigarette ash dropped into a dog's eye is an all too common accident. Wash the eye with a cool saline solution to rinse out the ash and clean the surface; then, if you have any ophthalmic ointment or penicillin ointment, squeeze a little into the eye before contacting the vet. Chemical burns resulting from splashing can be minimized by bathing with water. On the body, fur may prevent serious penetration but if the dog has walked into a puddle of acid or alkali some antidote should be administered. The animal may well have lapped up a little or licked its contaminated fur or paws. Inhaled fumes are another cause of internal chemical burns, which are very difficult to treat. If you work with dangerous chemicals or have them in the house for any reason find out what antidotes are suitable for both animals and humans and always keep them available in case of accident.

Swallowed Objects and Lodged Bones

Balls, toys, stones, pieces of wood, needles and thread—all kinds of things are swallowed. Sometimes they pass safely through the body and some may dissolve in the stomach fluids; but sometimes they demand an operation for their removal. If your dog is playing with something and then the object is nowhere to be found but the dog starts vomiting, you may suspect that it has been swallowed. Always discourage an animal from playing with something small enough to swallow or toys made of materials which can be chewed up into small pieces which could cause a blockage.

Bones and other objects sometimes become lodged across the mouth. They are best gripped with a pair of pliers and manoeuvred free whilst an assistant holds the dog's mouth open. Bone splinters passing into the digestive system can be dangerous, for their sharp points can pierce a tissue wall and lead to peritonitis. Give dogs only large bones to gnaw upon and remove them if they begin to splinter. Sometimes a dog will retch as though it had something stuck in its throat when there is nothing there. This may be a symptom of tonsillitis or bronchitis.

Parasites

Fleas have already been dealt with in the main text (pp 75–6) but there are several other parasites, external and internal, to which dogs play host. These include a variety of ticks and mites, worms and fungal infections of which the following are the ones most frequently encountered.

Mange

This is caused by a variety of mites which infest the skin causing irritation. It can become a very serious condition and is contagious to humans. If your dog shows signs of a diffuse, scaly skin condition, especially if coupled with hair loss, consult your vet.

Ear Mites

These can also be a problem. They are easily treated with an oil which your vet will prescribe but can produce a serious condition if their presence is unnoticed and they work their way into the inner ear. Symptoms are dirty ears, scratching and head shaking. The head is usually held to one side with the affected ear on the lower side. These symptoms can also indicate an ear inflammation caused by draughts, as with dogs that lean their heads out of car windows, or foreign bodies, such as grass seeds, invading the ear. Excessive head shaking may lead to a blood blister (haematoma) on the ear flap which may require surgery.

Ringworm

This is not a worm but a fungal infection, named for the circular blemish on the skin which can sometimes be seen, although it is often not readily visible except under ultraviolet light. It often develops first around the eyes, the gum line or the feet and can rapidly become serious, not least because it is transmissible to man. It can be easily treated with medicine but the animal then needs regular check-ups for a period to ensure that it is really clear of infection.

Lice and Ticks

These are more easily dealt with than other parasites. Lice can usually be seen as slow-moving white specks in the fur, often in clusters. Close inspection shows them to be light orange in colour. Although highly irritant they can be killed by parasiticidal baths or powders. Treat bedding, too. Ticks, which look like small black peas when engorged with blood, can be treated with parasiticidal baths but small infestations, usually around the eyes and mouth and in the ears, can be picked off by hand if each tick is first dabbed with methylated spirit which will kill it. Do not try to remove live ticks or the mouth part of the creature may stay embedded in the dog's skin and cause an abscess. Unfortunately, there will still be plenty of ticks in the place where your dog first caught them, reinfestation is frequent. There are tablets available from vets, although not all recommend them, which can be given to the dog and which will ensure that any tick that bites it will soon die.

Internal Worms

These are of two main kinds: tapeworms and roundworms. Roundworms are especially common in puppies, who may inherit them from their mother. If a puppy has a distended stomach, develops diarrhoea and loses weight, round-worms could be the cause. It may vomit them up or pass them in its faeces. Roundworms are longish and white to pale yellow in colour, round and often curled at the ends. Tapeworms have a flatter appearance and usually break off into segments, looking like grains of rice, which can sometimes be seen attached to the fur around the anus. They too cause diarrhoea, vomiting and loss of weight. Both types are easily treated by worm tablets, but get your vet to prescribe the right type and quantity for your dog if you are not already very experienced in the problem. If you have any doubts about whether the animal is suffering

from worms—or about which type of worm is responsible—take a sample of the dog's faeces to the surgery
with the dog. If one puppy in a litter is suffering from
worms the whole litter should be treated.

Main Canine Diseases

Distemper

A virus disease which is particularly dangerous between
the age of weaning and a puppy's first birthday, although
it can attack a dog at any age. Canine distemper kills 50 to
80 per cent of infected puppies. The first symptoms are
usually fever, a discharge from the eyes or nose, loss of
appetite and perhaps some vomiting. This develops into
pneumonia with diarrhoea, and the liver is affected. A
further development is 'hard pad', believed to be caused
by a mutation of the virus in which the foot pads are
enlarged and hardened, with the external nose tissue and
the eyelids also often being affected. The virus then goes
on to destroy the nervous system and even if it is arrested
at this stage the dog may throw fits for the rest of its life.
Fortunately, vaccines have been developed which provide
immunity to these diseases. While a puppy is being fed its
first milk (colostrum) by its mother many antibodies are
passed on which give the youngster a passive immunity,
provided that the mother is immune (either through having
recovered from the disease or through vaccination), but
this immunity wears off by about ten or twelve weeks of
age. The puppy should then be vaccinated and kept away
from other dogs for a couple of weeks to allow a build-up
of immunity. Booster doses will be needed regularly
throughout the dog's life according to your vet's advice. If
your dog has a great deal of contact with other dogs your
vet may consider that it gets sufficient exposure to the
general pool of disease not to require reimmunization.

Hepatitis

Known variously as Infectious Canine Hepatitis, Canine Virus Hepatitis or Rubarth's Disease, this is a condition affecting the liver. Fortunately, it is not very common, since the only initial signs are usually weakness, lethargy and weight loss. If handled, the dog will react as though the abdomen were tender. The dog develops a high temperature and will usually pant. In severe cases tonsillitis and conjunctivitis will probably be present and eventually jaundice may develop. This is a disease which affects mainly puppies, but can occur at any age. Incubation is from nine to ten days and sometimes, in mild cases, it may last only a few days and the animal will recover; sometimes, however, the progress of the disease is so rapid that the dog may die before anyone has realized that it is ill. A successful vaccine is available which can be combined with distemper vaccine and given at the same time.

Leptospirosis

A bacterial disease which is transmissible to man and to cats. It can be caught by oral or nasal contact with infected urine, by drinking infected water or by penetration of the tender skin between the toes when walking through contaminated puddles. Dogs may remain carriers long after they appear to have recovered. Symptoms are very close to those of hepatitis and distemper. Vaccines are available, usually administered combined in a triple shot with those for distemper and hepatitis, which should be boosted annually. In the US many consider it wiser to boost every six months.

Rabies

Also known as hydrophobia, this is one of the most terrible diseases known. For this reason Britain has strict quarantine regulations for all mammals brought into the country. This creates hardship for both pets and owners but is better than the risk of the disease itself. Any pet owner who tries to smuggle their dog into the country is totally misguided (apart from being liable to punishment which could include the destruction of the dog) for only by this strict imposition of the law are all dogs, cats, humans and other vulnerable species protected. A rabies vaccine does exist and is an essential precaution in countries where rabies is prevalent or at any time of risk. In lands with quarantine regulations, such as Britain, Eire, Australia and Hawaii, the situation is much safer, for no vaccine is 100 per cent effective and, anyway, who is going to vaccinate the millions of wild animals that would also be at risk and in turn be a likely threat to humans?

Transmission of the disease is usually through a bite, the virus being transferred with the carrier's saliva, but it can be through cuts or other open wounds. The first sign shown by the victim is a change of temperament: quiet dogs become fierce, aggressive ones quiet; by then the virus has already invaded the body and attacked the brain. In the next stage the dog appears to go mad, attacking everything in its path. Finally, paralysis overcomes the animal. In dogs, the whole process from first signs to death may last only a week. There is no cure but, because the only way in which the disease can be positively diagnosed is to study the brain of the dead animal for changes which do not show up until just prior to death, the dog ideally should not be put out of its misery: it should be trapped and restrained. However, if you think that you have a rabid dog *take no risks*: if it is necessary, shoot the animal. If you think you have been bitten by a rabid animal seek medical help immediately. Although no cure is yet known recovery is possible if treatment is started soon enough. Only after the animal's brain has been studied will it be possible correctly to assess your danger.

Remember, of course, to inform the police.

Keeping Your Dog in Trim

Grooming, beyond regular brushing and combing, will depend upon whether you are keeping your dog purely as a pet or whether you intend to show it, or at least make it conform to the show concept of the breed. Breed books and pamphlets may be available in your pet store giving detailed instructions for clips and trims, but the best way of finding out is from experts at breed shows. If you take your dog to a beauty parlour do not expect the staff to check its health or to treat any problems—that is your responsibility.

Dogs do not require frequent baths; twice a year is usually adequate. Always wet the dog's head last, for when its head is wet a dog will begin to shake itself dry. Always rinse soap out thoroughly and make sure that the dog is well dried. Do not let it go from a bath straight out into the cold—and, when you do let it out, do not be surprised if it immediately rolls in the dirt and is soon just as dirty as it was before! Never bathe a dog that is sick: wash it with a sponge or use a dry shampoo. Do not bathe puppies or pregnant bitches.

In some breeds it is traditional to shorten the tail by cutting if off (docking) or to trim the ears to a different shape by surgery (called cropping, and forbidden in Britain). There may be a practical reason for the first in certain working dogs but cosmetic surgery is otherwise only a matter of conforming to a human idea of what breeders would prefer a dog to look like. It is a matter of some controversy, although perhaps it may be considered only an extension of the interference by which man has already produced some of the more extreme breed characteristics.

Training Your Dog

Despite remarks in the earlier part of this book the important point about training your dog is that you do the training, for unless you are in control the man–dog relationship will not work. Naturally, all dogs cannot be trained to the same degree. Some breeds will have generations of instinctive behaviour bred into them, making them easier to teach to perform certain tasks. Some breeds seem to display rather faster thinking—this has been claimed for the Doberman, for instance—and others, such as the majority of hounds, tend to be slower on the uptake. Breed may also affect temperament: Alsatians (German shepherds) will tend to be strong-willed and need firm handling while breeds such as the Labrador retriever, especially the bitches, are usually of a gentle disposition. These things should be taken into account in the way you train and handle your dog but, whatever the traditional expectation for its type, you should base your methods on a close observation of the personality of the individual dog itself.

Calmness, patience, consistency and firmness are what you need to train a dog and have a happy, obedient companion. Decide what words you are going to use for particular instructions, make sure that they are short and clearly distinguished, then keep to them. Try to avoid using the dog's name when you are admonishing it, and never lose your temper however long it takes to get the dog to do your bidding. When it does, praise it and reward it with a display of pleasure and affection so that it knows it has done what is wanted. If you do find your temper beginning to get frayed during a training session, stop the lesson.

House-training has already been dealt with (Chapter 3). It is simply a matter of watching for the right moment and showing the puppy where to go, backed up by a timetable which enables it to keep to regular toilet times.

Stopping the dog from doing things such as sitting on chairs which it should not is a matter of admonishment, followed by removal if the dog does not remove itself, then praise for it being where it should be.

Getting a puppy used to a collar and then a lead does not usually cause problems if started when it is young. It will resist and tug at first but if you hold on it will soon decide to give up the struggle. Do not try to begin obedience training while it is still a very bouncy puppy, but do not leave it so late that bad habits have already become ingrained. Basic equipment that you will need consists of a choke chain, a lead and a length of line. Choose somewhere familiar to the dog but away from people and traffic as your training ground so that the dog is confident and will not be distracted. Have frequent lessons, daily if possible, and keep them short: twenty minutes will be quite enough. Do not proceed to a new order until you are confident that the earlier ones are mastered but always include all the earlier learning in each lesson to keep it fresh. Here is one way of teaching the basic instructions you will need:

Walking to Heel

This should be taught first. With the choke chain around the dog's neck and the lead attached place the dog to your left. Hold the lead in your *right* hand (left-handed people may reverse all these instructions), so that it hangs loosely across your body, and use your left hand to hold the lead firmly and as near the chain as possible for comfort. Make sure that the dog is placed with its front legs lined with your left leg, where you can see it easily and it can see your movements. Ready? Now walk in a straight line or in a very wide circle keeping the dog in the same position by control of the lead and your own pace. Talk to the dog and whenever it moves out of alignment say 'Heel!' loudly and clearly. (It doesn't matter what word you choose; choose another if you wish, provided that it is not one likely to be frequently heard in conversation, and then stick to it.) Do not jerk the dog back or drag it behind you. Be ready with a consistent pressure whenever it strays from position. If it stops completely, stop yourself, pat your leg, call it and say 'Heel'. Praise it when it comes. Do not be too downhearted if you seem to make no progress; break before

102

your patience becomes exhausted and try again next day. Equally, even if it works like magic, be prepared for slower progress later.

Turns

You have to teach your dog to stay close even when you change direction. Halt your progress to pivot on your left heel, meanwhile using your right leg to push the dog gently into a turn while repeating the word 'Heel'. Do not step off again until you have the dog in the right position and then walk on a distance before trying the move again. It is worth practising this operation without the dog to get it smooth on your part. When you are confident that this lesson has been mastered (but not in the same session) try doing the same for a right turn, using your left foot to guide the dog. When both turns are mastered try alternating the directions in which you walk, then organizing them randomly. Add the occasional turn back upon yourself, which will involve passing the lead behind your back to avoid it wrapping around your body.

When you are absolutely confident that your dog will stay at heel in whatever direction you walk try releasing it from the lead. This point will come when the dog is always in the correct position without your having to exert any pressure through the lead. Some people use the expedient of first allowing the dog to walk freely with its lead draped around its neck before removing it altogether.

Sit

With your dog back on the lead and walking correctly to heel come to a halt while gently pulling on the lead to raise your dog's head and prevent it from going on. Run your left hand down the animal's back, pushing its hindquarters down. Meanwhile, firmly say 'Sit!' and repeat the word several times. If it obeys praise it, but not effusively or it may rise again to show its pleasure. If it does, say 'Sit!' and push it down again. Walk on and repeat the exercise. Always give the dog a reasonable period of walking between the instructions to sit. Next, try stopping and going through the command and the motion of pushing the dog down without actually touching it. When the dog is regularly responding to this try to achieve the response by using the command alone or the hand movement alone. Soon the dog should be getting used to the idea that it should sit whenever you stop. When this has been achieved you can try working with the dog off the lead. At first use both the signal and command. If you are obeyed reduce it to only one of them and finally do it without the signals. Eventually you should have the dog walking close to heel and sitting whenever you stop. Nevertheless, do not take risks; even with a highly trained dog put it on a lead whenever you are out in busy streets with traffic.

Stay

So far you have been teaching the dog to stay with you. Now you have to teach it to go against this training when given the specific instruction 'Stay'. For the new lesson you must put it back on the lead again. By now it will probably have begun to associate the training place and the use of the choke chain and lead as linked with learning something new. Walk the dog to heel, halt and give the instruction to sit. Now turn to face the dog, repeating 'Sit!'; then, letting the lead go slack, raise your free hand, either with the palm flat or with the index finger raised, and give the instruction 'Stay!'. Walk backwards as far as the lead will allow without exerting pressure, continuing to repeat 'Stay!'. If the dog does not move return to it, take up your position beside it, make it walk to heel, halt and sit, walk and then try the lesson again. If the dog does not stay always go back to it, push it back to the sit position and give the instruction again. This is very confusing to the dog. It will almost certainly attempt to come with you at first. When it stays, praise it when you go back to it, not

104

from the distance or it will feel the urge to join you. After
it has learned to stay you must teach it to do so even when
you are out of sight. This lesson should repeat all it has
learned previously, but while it stays move in an arc to one
side of it. The dog will turn to look at you and when you
reach a point where you go out of its vision it will probably
get up. Stop, return to it and begin again, having instructed
it to sit and stay. When it has mastered that, move in an
arc in the opposite direction. Now attempt this while
circling the animal. Eventually, you can try the exercise
without the lead, but still go only a lead's distance away.

When you are sure that the dog thoroughly under-
stands, you can gradually increase the distance to which
you go. When you reach about twenty yards from the dog
you can change the pattern, but always remember to return
to the dog to give it praise. Never call it to you. Now you
can walk off to the side, or eventually directly to the dog's
rear. Some trainers suggest that in no circumstances should
you call a dog to you from the stay, but always return to it.
This ensures that it waits confident of your return and is
not always eagerly anticipating your call to join you.

Here

As always, go back to the chain and lead and repeat
previous exercises when you begin a new lesson. Although
many people will use the word 'Here!' or 'Come!' to call
their dog to them there is no need since 'Heel' already
means 'Stay close to me'—and anyway sounds rather like
'Here'. Take the exercise as far as the already learned
'Stay' and from the full length of lead call the dog to heel.
If it does not respond pull gently on the lead, repeating
the command. Do not drag the dog towards you; just
exert a gentle tug and then take up the slack as the dog
joins you. When this is fully learned, lengthen the lead
with string or cord and increase the distance involved.
When the dog is working satisfactorily over a distance of
about twenty yards abandon the cord and lead, although

go back to short distances at first, gradually increasing the space between you and the dog.

When you are confident of the dog's reaction introduce some distraction in the form of other people (but do not take the risk of going out into a street with traffic or a busy public place).

Stop

Once again you need to work with collar, lead and cord. If your dog is so well trained that he never leaves your side when out then get someone else to call the dutiful animal to them. Hold the cord at a length of about three or four yards and, when the dog has almost reached that distance, call out 'Stop!' so that the pressure is applied to halt the dog as the cord reaches its full extent. If the dog turns to return to you tell it to stay. If it obeys go to it and give it some praise. Gradually extend the distance at which you stop the dog as you repeat the exercise. When you feel confident of the dog's obedience coil the cord on the ground and use your foot to put pressure upon it and halt the dog. Eventually perform the exercise—short distances at first and then with the dog further away from you— without lead and cord. This command is invaluable in preventing an animal both from running into danger and from chasing animals, people or vehicles as well as for halting it when it misbehaves.

Obedience to these basic commands will enable you to control your dog in the majority of circumstances. When the dog is totally obedient to them all you may perhaps begin to call your dog to you from a 'Stay' or 'Stop' position but always be certain that you will not be putting the animal at risk from traffic or any other dangers and do not call it if in doing so you would be asking it to do anything which you have already established as forbidden.

Once a dog has learned these basic exercises you can go on to teach it a whole variety of games and tricks, or professional tasks if it is to be a working dog. Most dogs will happily chase a rolled or thrown ball or stick. When they have picked it up call them to you. If they do not naturally go and pick things up wait until they do it by chance and use that as the point to begin training. If a dog does not drop the ball or stick or allow you to remove it from his mouth without resistance do not force it from him; it will think this is another form of game, like tug-of-war. Grasp the ball or stick in one hand and pull the dog away from it.

You can teach jumping over objects, or even through hoops, calling the dog with the obstacle blocking its path, placed very low at first, then gradually higher as you repeat the exercise on later occasions.

Sophisticated obedience training and the training of working dogs is probably best done with the help of professional trainers. Your local police station will probably be able to tell you where the nearest obedience classes are held or you can enquire through the Kennel Club.

Showing Your Dog

If you want to compete in dog shows visit some to see what they are like and how they are organized. You will find announcements of British shows regularly published in the weekly journals called *Dog World* and *Our Dogs* which you can order from your newsagent, or in the Kennel Club's *Kennel Gazette*. The American Kennel Club publishes lists of shows in its magazine *Pure Bred Dogs*.

Some Useful Addresses

The Kennel Club,
1 Clarges Street,
London, W.1.

Canine Defence,
10 Seymour Street,
London, W.1.

The Blue Cross Society,
1 Hugh Street,
London, S.W.1.

The People's Dispensary for
Sick Animals,
PDSA House, South Street,
Dorking, Surrey.

The Royal Society for the
Prevention of Cruelty to
Animals, The Manor House,
Horsham, Sussex.

American Kennel Club,
51 Madison Avenue,
New York, NY 10010.

Australian National Kennel
Council,
Royal Show Grounds,
Ascot Vale, Victoria.

Canadian Kennel Club,
111 Eglinton Avenue,
Toronto 12, Ontario.

New Zealand Kennel Club,
P.O. Box 523,
Wellington 1.

Kennel Club of Southern
Africa,
P.O. Box 562,
Cape Town.

The American Society for
the Prevention of Cruelty
to Animals,
441 E 92nd Street,
New York, NY 10028

The Humane Society of
the United States,
1604 K Street NW,
Washington, DC, 20006.

INDEX